Earl G. Long

To Bill Jenkins
My fellow "islander"
All good wishes
Earl Long
9-VI-95

Longman Group Limited,
Longman House, Burnt Mill, Harlow,
Essex CM20 2JE, England
and Associated Companies throughout the world

Carlong Publishers (Caribbean) Limited
PO Box 489
Kingston 10

33 Second Street
Newport West
Kingston 13, Jamaica

Longman Trinidad Limited
Boundary Road
San Juan
Trinidad

Copp Clark Longman Ltd.
2775 Matheson Blvd East
Mississauga
Ontario L4W 4P7
Canada

Longman Publishing Group
10 Bank Street
White Plains
New York 10601–1951, USA

First published 1994

British Library Cataloguing in Publication Data
A CIP record for this book is available from the British Library

Series Editor

Stewart Brown

Set in Baskerville

Produced through Longman Malaysia

ISBN 0 582 23913.3

To Sharon, Jeremy, Albert, Madeleine, Paula, Keturah, Alma, Roger, Glenn, Lauren, Lynden and Albert Jr, and to the people of Mon Repos.

Author's Acknowledgements

Nora Day, Jeanne Ridley, Robert Lee and Stewart Brown pushed, prodded and advised to make *Consolation* possible.

Chapter 1

It is a place where the villages are blessed with names like Patience and Repose; where two bays are called Great Hole and Little Hole; and where a peninsula, pointing forever across the Atlantic to Africa, is called Cinnamon. The people are gentle like the names they give to their small pieces of hillside and riverbank. They are too poor to stop loving, so they give their love as familiar names to those they know, to strangers and to the land. The land in return, although perennially thirsty, gives back all it can, and that is just enough.

If one had come by sea to Great Hole, and landed at the middle of the beach, and looked up the valley that spread its arms in welcome, one would have seen a bend in the road that went through the village of Consolation. At the outside of the arc was a small white and green house, with a water tank to one side that shone like a silver cube. The colours of the house remained as a hint and were better seen from a distance, as Estephan St. Pierre had not repainted it since he had helped to build it fifty-four years earlier.

A narrow path led from the bay to the main road. It was difficult to see from the beach, as it constantly changed to seek the easiest route around fallen logs, rocks, and mud holes.

Bertrand Louis turned the key in a lock that would not have resisted a touch of wind, and walked along the last fifty feet of the path that led from the bay to the paved road. He was on his way to visit his best friend and to show respect. When he had come to the village twenty-one years ago, already an old man, with a worn cardboard suitcase and no history, the people had accepted him. Just as they had always accepted the sick, the orphaned and stray dogs. He knew many long words, and since the words came easily, the villagers showed him respect. Two other men walked together along the main road, just ahead of Bertrand Louis. They, too, were going to visit Estephan St. Pierre. The two were born in the same year, but because Maurice Jacob had worked ten hours a day, six days a week for most of his life, moulding and coaxing the soil, he looked twenty years younger than his companion. Serges Jean-Baptiste tried valiantly to keep up with his good friend. Bee-keeping did not equip a man to walk with another who thought that a place that could be reached only by a twenty-mile walk through scrub and swamps and over hills was 'just over there'. Occasionally, Maurice Jacob would pause for his friend, and Serges Jean-Baptiste, draped in an old khaki suit that had defeated time, strong soap and red-hot irons, would smile gratefully and urge his legs to go a little more quickly.

The three men who walked slowly up the hill to visit Estephan St. Pierre came in the evenings. They came when the sun had just set and the cooler night was rushing in, urged on by crickets and tree frogs impatient to begin their matings. Saturdays were the best days as people returning from shopping in the capital brought news. And on a Saturday evening in June, one week before he died of cancer of the prostate, Estephan St. Pierre watched his friends approaching and decided at last to love his wife.

At that moment, Simone St. Pierre was sitting behind the counter of a small shop set fifty feet south of the galvanized iron water tank. On her lap she balanced a plate of boiled salt codfish, cassava and avocado. Before each bite, she dabbed the food with a portion of a yellow pepper strong enough to peel the skin from a man's hand. The two dogs that sat at her feet, already burdened with the names Jesse James and Breadcrust, resigned themselves to gulping down the burning scraps she threw them, as the alternative was the even greater pain of an empty stomach.

Thirty-five years ago, Simone Marie-Claude La Forêt had

married Estephan St. Pierre when her father, Christopher Napoleon, had told her to. And on her wedding day, she saw her husband for the third time and spoke to him for the second time in her life.

Simone La Forêt had been sitting on a flat rock on the bank of the Consolation River with her two younger sisters and an aunt, when she encountered Estephan St. Pierre for the first time. The women were unaware of his presence on a malevolent looking grey horse standing where a narrow road paused at the river. His sonorous voice startled and frightened them and Simone sat paralyzed with fear, as one in the path of a rock slide, when his words thundered over her.

'Laure La Forêt has given the world a beautiful daughter. You could make a man cry,' he said, then spurred his horse across the river towards her home. He did not look back.

When he had disappeared, the aunt, Suzette Raquil said, 'Estephan St. Pierre thinks the world is his estate.' Then, looking directly at Simone, she added, 'You will have trouble with this man.'

The sixteen-year-old Simone La Forêt stood up suddenly and rushed to some low bushes to relieve the burning urgency of a suddenly full bladder. Her face burned with shame and anger at the man whose eyes had laughed at her and whose voice had violated her innocence. When she returned to her seat, her lips tight and her eyes narrowed, Simone La Forêt was no longer a child. While the sisters giggled, Suzette Raquil smiled in sympathy and sorrow for the beautiful niece she had just lost.

It was two days before Simone La Forêt's curiosity overcame her embarrassment to ask about Estephan St. Pierre.

'You think he'll come back? The man at the river.' Simone asked her aunt.

'Estephan St. Pierre?'

'Yes, you told me I would have trouble with him.'

Suzette Raquil smiled, trying to keep the mischief out of her eyes.

'Well, it may be good trouble,' she said.' The St. Pierres are the ones who put their name on this valley and the coast. They own most of Consolation. Listen child, Estephan St. Pierre knows he can get any woman in Consolation or in Two Hills.'

'I thought he was going to wipe his feet on us,' Simone said.

'A lot of women would like him to do that,' Suzette Raquil replied, knowing that Estephan St. Pierre's arrogance was expected and appreciated by his neighbours: humility was best left to those with no land or property.

'Your father probably sent word to St. Pierre that he had a daughter ready to be married. Why else would he have ridden alone to Two Hills?' Suzette Raquil said.

'Aunt 'Zette, I cannot marry that man. I do not even know him.' Simone was thoroughly alarmed, but the remembrance of the tall man on the grey horse made her wet herself again.

Estephan St. Pierre visited three months later, this time on a black horse that seemed ready to murder its rider and every living thing around it. One Sunday morning, when the family had returned from High Mass, the youngest sister rushed breathlessly into the kitchen, where Simone was peeling green bananas, and whispered excitedly, 'The same man by the river is here!'

For the third time Simone felt the moistness returning and she had to sit to continue her work and to force her breathing back to regularity.

Her mother came into the kitchen, her face expressionless. 'Put that down. Go and change.'

An hour later her mother came into the bedroom. 'Your father wants you to serve the guest.' Simone went into the small porch where the two men sat. Estephan St. Pierre was seated precariously on the edge of a small bench, fidgeting with a white Panama hat. His discomfort seemed to gratify her father, who was revelling in the honour paid him by a St. Pierre asking rather than demanding.

'This is Estephan St. Pierre,' he said in introduction. 'He has come to ask my permission to marry you. I have said yes.' Then turning to his guest, he said, 'A small punch?'

Estephan St. Pierre smiled and nodded at Simone. 'Please,' he said.

Simone returned to the kitchen, thinking of what she was sent to do, forcing out all thought of the calamity she faced. Her hand trembled so much that Laure La Forêt had to help her pour the rum and squeeze the juice from a lime into each glass. Simone added a teaspoon of sugar to each drink, then stirred slowly. She looked around the kitchen; all the old pots, so familiar that they had become friends and could not be thrown out. All the old smells of coconut oil, dried fish and unfinished wood would now be left behind. But the family had a guest, so she could not cry.

'It was the same with me,' her mother said, 'and I got a good husband.'

'But the man is a stranger,' Simone said accusingly.

'Estephan St. Pierre is a good man,' Laure La Forêt said, her forced resignation acknowledging the inevitability of an early marriage for her first daughter, whose beauty had allowed her father the privilege of choosing her husband. It was better that their daughter should marry a good man and go to heaven than to live with someone she chose and go to hell after a lifetime of happiness.

Christopher Napoleon La Forêt was satisfied that Father Alphonse, their parish priest, who wore black even when the sun melted the pitch road, would approve of his skilful match-making. So he rewarded himself with four glasses of rum punch.

The tired and bewildered old priest from Toulouse, who had been abandoned in the valley of St. Pierre, had avenged his exile by terrorizing the inhabitants of Consolation and three neighbouring villages with his detailed images of hell. His enthusiasm had not carried over to describing the joys of heaven, but his parishioners assumed that it was a better place than they had now.

Later, Simone was commanded to accompany her suitor to his tethered horse. As he replaced the saddle, she looked closely at the tall man, no longer arrogant but sweating profusely from the heat, rum and a flannel jacket. When the hawk-like face, moulded by the genes of Africans, Europeans and Caribs, turned towards her, she felt a sudden pity for the drunk and nervous man and, suddenly, she was a woman looking at the husband she would someday have to nurse. She reached out hesitantly and touched his hand.

He nodded and, as he strained to hold back the horse that had enough of him and the heat and the strange surroundings, said, 'You are so beautiful . . . you make me want to cry'.

Simone La Forêt smiled. She would marry Estephan St. Pierre. To her surprise, he succeeded in mounting his horse and managed to remain seated while the half-crazed beast bolted away, snapping small branches from an avocado tree. Simone thought that the diminishing thunder of hooves reminded her of her fiancé's rumble of a voice, and she returned to a family gathered on the small porch, smiling and crying.

On Saturday, June 2nd 1945, at eleven o'clock in the morning, Estephan St. Pierre married Simone La Forêt.

Preparations for the wedding had begun two weeks before; six months after Estephan had asked for Simone's hand. Elfrida St. Pierre, Estephan's housekeeper and second cousin, who had lived with him since the death of his parents from malaria, was initially responsible for the purchase of food and drink for the festivities. After two days, these burdens sent Elfrida to bed with a fever and blinding headaches. Madame Ferdinand, whose first name was unknown, but who had once travelled abroad and was considered very sophisticated, immediately assumed Elfrida's duties and more. She had extracted a solemn promise from the small orchestra that was to provide the dance music: the four members would remain sober until the guests started leaving.

Madame Ferdinand arranged with the owner of Consolation Reliable Transport for the groom and his entourage to be delivered safely and on time to the church at Two Hills. Charles Giraud, the owner, immediately made a great show of checking under the hood of the company's only vehicle – a Wells Fargo bus of unknown age – and, with a voice shaking with remorse, asked whether he was not famed for punctuality. Madame Ferdinand gazed in astonishment at Giraud for a moment, then walked away without another word.

Estephan St. Pierre's party would indeed be brought to the priest from Toulouse only fifteen minutes late.

Father Alphonse looked at the tall man with the profile of a benign hawk, and at the beautiful slight girl sitting in the next aisle, and felt a pinch of long-buried envy. He resolved to be especially brutal in his description of the punishment meted out to those who broke the sacred vows of marriage. When Simone La Forêt lifted her eyes for a brief moment, she caught the eyes of the priest and saw a grey, painful loneliness stretching far beyond the church and the valley. She shuddered and quickly looked down at her shoes.

The timid look from the girl evoked a small twinge of pity from the priest, but when he imagined her writhing and screaming in sinful ecstasy later that night, his pity changed rapidly to revulsion, and he once again sought refuge in thoughts of perdition.

When he rose to perform the wedding ceremony, he was overcome by the warm, thick smell of lime cologne, camphor, sweat and vetiver. He looked at all those happy and expectant faces and suddenly felt inadequate. He no longer wanted to talk of sin and divine retribution. He wanted to thank these people for having welcomed and sheltered and protected him. And the gaunt, unhappy, grey-eyed Frenchman wanted to die there; there in the valley of St. Pierre among the people who were too wise to reflect his resentment, but who had conquered him with patience and caring.

For the first time the parishioners of Consolation and Two Hills saw their priest smile, and a quick whisper ran through the church: they were witnesses to a special moment.

An hour and a half later, Estephan St. Pierre stood at the door of the small church with his bride and wondered whether his thirty years had prepared him for the greatest terror he had ever known. He marvelled that the sixteen-year-old girl had been able to sign her name while his hand had trembled so much that it had taken him most of a minute to write his.

The Consolation Reliable Transport had to make three trips between the church and Estephan's home. None of the two hundred guests had been sent an invitation, but it was understood that any absence would have caused regret and hurt.

Elfrida St. Pierre had recovered sufficiently to follow Madame Ferdinand around, organizing tables of food and drink, but was crying so powerfully that Madame Ferdinand had to warn her not to stand near the cake.

It had been necessary for the groom to provide only rum and brandy. Relatives and friends had cooked and brought white and yellow yams, rice, plantains, sweet potatoes, tanias and several bean sauces. There were huge cast-iron pots of mutton, beef, pork and chicken. Two large basins held a salad of cabbage, tomato, lettuce and boiled carrots. Elfrida and Madame Ferdinand squeezed in bowls of fried ripe plantains and sliced hearts of palm. The wedding cake, covered in white icing and silver beads, sat serenely in the middle of the main dining table, the target of frequent cries of admiration and wonder.

Many ponderous and wandering speeches were made,

and none were remembered. But when one speaker advised the bride, 'Remember not to take everything lying down,' Maurice Jacob asked, in a whisper that carried around the room, 'So she should take it all standing up?'

It was two days before Estephan St. Pierre was able to sleep in bed with his wife. The last guest did not leave until Monday evening.

That night, Simone discovered that the giggling, whispered lessons from older girls at school, on what men and women did together in bed, had not adequately prepared her for the humiliation of having her clothes brusquely removed by an older man who had become her husband before becoming her friend. As she lay trembling beneath his weight, she was thankful for the darkness and the smell of the old roses that the wind brought into the house.

For the rest of her life Simone St. Pierre would seek the solace of the old rose bushes whenever she was troubled. The roses had flourished in the south corner of the garden, near the water tank, for so long that no one could remember who had planted them. Their scent had penetrated every part of the house so deeply that visitors would always associate Simone and Estephan with the smell of roses.

Estephan St. Pierre was worried when his wife did not become pregnant within a year of their marriage. When another year had passed with no change in Simone's condition, he grew alarmed and persuaded her to see the doctor from the capital who came to the village clinic on Saturdays. Again Simone suffered the humiliation of being handled by a man who was doing what he had to do. When she informed him that she had been a virgin before marriage and had never experienced any burning or discharge 'down there', the doctor advised that her husband visit the clinic the next Saturday.

Simone St. Pierre was right when she suspected that her husband would not be pleased to hear the cause of their childlessness could be with him. Estephan waited until she had changed out of the good dress she had worn to the clinic.

'Simone,' he asked, 'what did the doctor say?'

'It may be you.'

'What are talking about?' he asked, trying to suppress the anger that was beginning to burn his face. 'Did you see the doctor? You're not lying to me, girl?'

But when he looked at the small, frightened girl who went to sit near the old roses, he could not convince himself that she could lie.

'That doctor doesn't know bullshit,' he muttered. 'The government sends only the worst ones to the country. If I go to a doctor, I'll go to a good one in town.'

The thought that a St. Pierre could not father children was so ludicrous to Estephan that he wondered why he had felt any anger or concern. But he hesitated to go to the doctor. After two months, his wife's brief accusing glances had weakened his resolve not to see the doctor.

He arrived at the clinic shortly before the end of clinic hours. Three women with children and an old man waiting on a bench outside the clinic door were glad to show their respect for Estephan St. Pierre by insisting that he see the doctor before them. Estephan repaid their courtesy by insisting that one woman, with a child whose lips were cracked with fever and who was wet with sweat, go in before him. This pause also gave him an opportunity to assure the others that he felt quite well but thought that everyone should visit the doctor at least once a year. The old man nodded in agreement and said he wished he could have done so, but there had been no doctors to come to the clinics until ten years ago. The women said that if the children were not having fever, then they were having diarrhoea, and so they had to visit the clinic at least once a month anyway.

For the first time in his adult life, Estephan St. Pierre stood nearly naked before another man. It was even worse than being completely naked, as he had been asked only to drop his trousers and underwear. He stood holding up his shirt, his eyes fixed on a chart on the wall too far way to read, and his nostrils narrowed to escape the sour, butyric smell of nervous perspiration that seemed to come from every pore. He was embarrassed for the doctor and wished he had doused himself in cologne. It was only when the doctor asked him to dress that he discovered that he had been holding his breath, and he was doubly grateful for the comfortable warmth of his trousers and the abatement of pain in his chest. The doctor, who had scarcely touched him, went to wash his hands and, while he was drying them, seemed suddenly to remember something and asked:

'Did you ever have mumps?'

'Yes,' said Estephan.

'How old were you then?'

Estephan paused, 'It was three years after leaving school. Fifteen . . . yes fifteen.'

'Did you have pain and swelling in your groin while your throat was swollen?'

'No,' said Estephan, 'it was a little later, about two weeks.'

'Mr. St. Pierre,' said the doctor, 'we will never know for certain, but that sickness may be the reason you cannot have a child.'

Estephan St. Pierre fought to keep his bowels from opening. He felt alternating waves of heat and cold wash down his body and his feet, which now felt very cold and heavy and would not move.

'I'm sorry,' the doctor said and glanced at the door; the visit was over.

As Estephan entered the waiting room, the young nurse looked up, smiling helpfully.

'Everything's all right?' she asked.

'I'll endure,' said Estephan, forcing a slight smile. Why did she have to look at him? How could she miss the shame in his eyes? He wanted to rush outside, but she continued.

'Tell Simone good-day for me. My name's Antoinette. We knew each other at school. She's well?'

'Yes. Very well,' said Estephan, beginning to hate his well-meaning torturer. 'I'll tell her. Take care of yourself.'

'Goodbye, Mr. St. Pierre,' said the nurse, happy to have given a little joy to another patient. 'Carry yourself well.'

The deprivations caused by the world war continued for five years. Then flour, fabrics and canned goods again became available. Simone St. Pierre persuaded Estephan to sell nine acres of farmland and to build a small shop. She had rightly concluded that she could save the villagers a day-long trip to the capital to shop for basic necessities, and the people of Consolation showed their gratitude by paying her extortionate prices. Simone prospered. Within a year, Estephan St. Pierre's participation in commerce was limited to carrying boxes of goods from Charles Giraud's new truck to the shop.

And the end of the war, which had been the impetus for Estephan St. Pierre to marry, did not bring him peace. A disease during his adolescence had left him half a man, and his wife had gently but quickly taken her independence.

Simone St. Pierre accepted her husband's withdrawal as she had accepted most things – without comment or rebellion. If Estephan no longer reached for her at night, then it was probably because he was too tired from fighting the sea and the forest and the crops. Mornings, at the first suspicion of dawn, Simone would be summoned from bed by the crowing of every insomniac and priapic cock in the neighbourhood, to the small kitchen behind the shop to prepare breakfast. It never varied – small cups of coffee, thick and sweet as molasses, and a small loaf lathered with salty oleomargarine. And while it was still dark, Estephan sharpened a machete, filled an empty rum bottle with drinking water, and put into an enamelled saucepan a lump of salt-meat, onions and a pat of oleomargarine; sometimes a loaf of bread.

There was seldom news for conversation. The village was sheltered from news of events which caused men to murder each other and to launch ships that could carry more people than all the inhabitants of the St. Pierre Valley. If great discoveries would benefit the villagers of Consolation, then they would come in time. The younger ones would introduce the new things, and the old people, after a proper interval of protest, warning and rejection, would accept the new things too. Life was preparation for heaven, and hard physical work would bring most necessities; otherwise, God would provide. So Estephan would leave every morning, except Sunday, with the same farewell.

'Good, I'm leaving now.' It was a ritual announcement since Simone did not have to be present. If she did hear, her response was always the same.

'Look after yourself.'

Ten years after it had come to an end, the war caused its first casualty in Consolation and made Estephan St. Pierre a man deserving of respect.

Frederick Albin had been the first in his village to attend the secondary school in the capital. With the single-minded relentlessness with which his people cultivated the soil, Frederick Albin devoured his studies. There was neither joy nor resent-ment in his attitude towards learning, just a willingness to remember everything he heard or read. But the village boy, unaware that he was expected to acquire city habits, neglected to lose the accent, smell and clothes of the country. After graduation, despite grades that were too good to elicit envy, his lack of influential friends or patrons condemned him to a low-paying job in the treasury.

When the British colonial authorities asked for volunteers to fight for Mother England, Frederick Albin registered.

And on one of the most memorable days of their history, half of the population of Consolation assembled at the harbourside, bearing pillows, fruits, dried meat, clothes, canned food and packed suitcases for the son who would bring so much honour to their village – the only one of them who would set eyes on King George and Queen Elizabeth.

But his letters, which came from European countries that only the priest and schoolmaster had heard of, did not prepare the villagers for the aged, limping, gaunt and wild-eyed figure who came back, armed only with a dirty duffel bag. Frederick Albin was unable to understand why the people he had fought for had despised him even more than they did the enemy. For most of the war, he had been forced to do menial tasks with other black men with strange accents and habits. And, when it was over, he was told, in words fashioned to dissemble, that he was not welcome. A shattered knee was repaired sufficiently, his severance pay was sent to a bank account at home, and a too-quick handshake thanked and discharged him.

Frederick Albin arrived unexpectedly one night on a government public-works truck. The smell of burning firewood and cooking, the calls of parents and children, the territorial challenges of village mongrels – all threatened to overwhelm and suffocate him. He wanted to call at each home and shout that he was back and would never leave them again; that he had never loved them enough, and that they must never stop touching and holding him. But his knee burned and he was so tired.

He knocked softly on the door of his old home, trying to hold back the crying and to withstand the pain from a heart beating so hard that it hurt his chest and head.

'Who is the person?' his father's voice said.

'I've arrived,' replied Frederick Albin.

The people of Consolation poured their love on Frederick, as generously as only those with little wealth can do. In time, they came to learn that too much closeness made him uncomfortable, and they reluctantly gave him some aloneness, too. The English manager of the largest estate near St. Pierre Valley hired him as a book-keeper, and Frederick Albin joined the priest and schoolmaster as an educated man of the village.

Estephan St. Pierre had just returned home from his farm one evening, and was unloading the pannier from a donkey, when a boy came running towards him, screaming in terror.

'Mr. Estephan! Quick! Mr. Frederick's killed the boss!'

'Simone! Trouble! I'm going to see Frederick!' he cried, and ran off to saddle the grey horse.

Most of the village seemed to have gathered near the main house of the estate. Frederick Albin stood outside the door of an annexe that served as his office. He was holding a bloody machete and shouting at someone who was locked inside. The estate owner had called Frederick a monkey, and Frederick, who had endured so many insults in Europe, had been unable to suffer another insult by a European in this small country that was his own. So Frederick had rushed outside and grabbed a machete from a worker cutting the grass nearby, and he had lashed out at the Englishman trying to run from the office. The man had managed to get back into the office and to close the door, but not before receiving a long shallow cut across his chest.

Someone had been dispatched to fetch the police, but the small station was six miles away; it would take the police more than an hour to arrive.

Frederick was hacking wildly at the door and muttering insanely. When he looked at the crowd he seemed unable to recognize anyone. He ignored all entreaties to stop and swung at two men who had crept up slowly to try and disarm him. The estate owner's wife was sitting on the grass, staring fixedly at the deranged man and rocking back and forth, whimpering. The village women, so ready to give comfort, stood uneasily near the white woman, ready to protect and comfort her but restrained by her foreignness and because her husband's attacker was one of their own.

His horse had sensed the fear in the crowd, and was becoming more difficult to control, so Estephan St. Pierre tethered him to the trunk of a coconut tree out of sight of the disturbance. Through the screams of the children and the low, urgent, disparate murmurs of people helplessly witnessing a catastrophe, Estephan could hear the dull thud of a machete biting into wood and the occasional scream of metal as the blade struck a nail or hinge. The villagers, desperate to share the burden of their horror, quickly crowded around Estephan.

'He's gone mad!'

'The white man is still alive!'

'We can't get near him!'

'What are we going to do?'

'Someone's gone to get the police.'

'Estephan, disbelieving that he could be harmed by the distraught man who seemed intent on murder, walked towards his friend.

'Frederick,' he called softly, then more loudly.

Frederick spun around as though startled. His eyes held no sign of recognition.

'Don't come near me, I'll kill you too,' said the strange, harsh voice.

'It's me, Estephan . . . Estephan, your friend,' said Estephan, terrified by the hating eyes and the transformed voice.

He wanted to run back to the crowd, but the thought of the consequent shame stopped him.

'No more, Frederick, no more, please. Come, let's go home now.'

A look of bewilderment appeared on Frederick Albin's face as he walked slowly towards Estephan.

'Mr. St. Pierre?' he asked softly, then dropped the machete.

‘Estephan St. Pierre put his arms around the younger man and the two sat on the low step near the door, and Estephan wept for the loss of the children’s innocence, for the destruction of their village’s favourite son, and for the act that had caused blood to be spilled.

Mason Thorpe refused to come out of the office until the police arrived. His wife eventually persuaded him to let her in, and the two sat behind the barricaded door until the police inspector and a corporal arrived in a long Land Rover. The corporal first drove the wounded man and his wife to the small clinic, then took the Inspector, a terrified and trembling Frederick Albin, Estephan and three witnesses to the Police Station. The Inspector made no effort to place handcuffs on Frederick, but he locked the machete in a metal box beneath the left bench-seat.

Frederick Albin spent the next five years in the mental hospital in the capital. His father died of grief eighteen months after the incident, convinced that he had failed his son. His mother never again entered the small village church after her husband’s funeral. She could not believe that there could exist a God capable of such cruelty to those He professed to love.

Three days after the incident, there was a story in the only national newspaper. The title read, ‘Farmer Saves Englishman’s Life.’ It did not matter that Estephan had not uttered a single one of the words attributed to him, but he carefully cut out the story and placed the strip with his most important documents. No one else in the village had ever received such honour.

During the next two years, Estephan St Pierre became god-father to fifteen of the children born in the village; and Simone, godmother to seven of these. It also became customary to seek Estephan’s advice on major decisions or at least to ensure that he was informed. In time, Estephan came to see these things not as courtesies, but as obligations.

Chapter 2

Bertrand Louis had been a good son because of his father's strong right arm and a leather belt. So Bertrand raised his children, Lise and Nicholas, on a foundation strengthened by belts, rulers and switches cut from a tamarind tree. With diligence and regularity, he impressed the virtues of respect, obedience, hard work and faith on the skin of his children, a skill acquired as the headmaster of a private school of thirty pupils.

The one-room school of St. Boniface was the converted home of Bertrand's parents. It served the small community at the southern edge of the capital, where the city seemed too tired to climb any more hills. In his shingled domain, with the help of two elementary school graduates, Bertrand Louis taught his charges that the earth was round, that rain was water falling from the sky, and that God made man to love Him, to serve Him and to be happy with Him forever in the next life. He was fair to all by ensuring that each received some punishment during the day, and he was especially careful to demonstrate that his own children did not receive preferential treatment.

For Lise and Nicholas, Mondays to Fridays were days of assured pain; Saturdays provided occasional relief, and on Sundays the two children begged the saints, especially St. Anthony of Padua, to protect them from their parents' love.

In later years, the children would wonder why they had been whipped for playing in their own backyard or giggling in bed. And Celine, their mother, would probably have been amazed and relieved to learn that children could be raised to be dutiful citizens without the aid of constant flagellation.

Celine Louis was a good woman. Every Sunday, at two o'clock in the afternoon, she heaped food on two aluminium plates – kept separate from the other dishes – for two of the town's derelicts. The two men, struggling resolutely to hide the effects of a breakfast of white rum, would walk quietly to the back door of the schoolmaster's house and knock softly. On good days, they were allowed to sit on the steps to eat, but when it rained, Celine would provide pieces of cardboard to cover the food and they were expected to find some other sheltered place. Bertrand Louis was confident that the ledgers of heaven would note that he fully approved of his wife's charity.

As Lise grew older, her parents, and especially her father, noticed that she did not exude the sharp smells of puberty, but continued to smell like a baby. At fifteen, Lise Louis's body smelled like the wind that came from the forests on the hillside in the mornings. Those who had lived all their lives in the city did not recognize her scent, although it disturbed men powerfully. The people who came from the country knew that perfume intimately; and one day, an old lady, who walked six miles from her village every day to sell tomatoes and herbs door-to-door, said to Lise, 'Little girl, you smell like forest water.'

Lise, aware that she was not especially beautiful, but unaware of her body's perfume, did not understand why her nearness caused men's nostrils to flare and their hands to be constantly caressing her shoulders. Her father began beating her more violently and under the slightest pretext, as he grew increasingly perturbed by the pull of her scent and by his revulsion at being attracted to his daughter.

One evening, after he had heard Lise singing a calypso that he did not approve of, Bertrand beat her so severely that Celine had had to push him away and warn him that, from that day on, she alone would discipline their daughter, or she would send Lise to her sister Solange.

Nicholas, who had benefited from the attention paid by his father to Lise, now found himself repelled by girls who smelled as they should, and not of forest water. At fourteen, the slender, subdued boy found more comfort in the attention of older boys and men than in the provocations of adolescent girls.

In the month of December, 1956, a small thing came to the country; a thing so small that it could not be imagined. But the invisible, invincible miasma spread from lung to lung, tying thousands to their beds with influenza. Then the staphylococcal bacteria, which had provoked the pustules on the legs of children, burrowed into the sick lungs and turned them raw and bloody.

Bertrand Louis watched his wife's dying stretch through nine days. Even after her funeral, he went home expecting to find her frying fish for supper. The two derelicts, who had been kept alive by Celine's kindness, had followed the funeral cortege at a distance so that they would not embarrass the procession. Each had managed to find a clean white shirt, and they walked carefully with forced sobriety, their eyes wide with terror and grief. They had lost the good woman who had cared.

Celine's death warned of the end of an old life. The face of the world was assuming new expressions that Bertrand could not begin to understand: when the Russians threw their satellite beyond the sky, he was unable to explain to himself or his pupils why the metal ball did not immediately fall to earth. His mortification grew even heavier when he overheard an eleven-year-old pupil spell the name of the United Nations Secretary General to a benchmate: he, the headmaster, could not.

'H-a-m-m-a-r-s-k-j-o-l-d!' the child had said triumphantly.

So words and happenings that previously had been the province of the British Broadcasting Corporation came to St. Boniface School at the bottom of the hill, where the city stopped.

Now that their measure of civility had been taken away, the bewildered and frightened family of Bertrand Louis searched for new interactions, but each asked too much of the others. Requests became demands, apologies became insults, and short sharp words were thrown with such vehemence that, even when they were taken back, the lacerations they had caused continued to bleed.

No experience or exercise could have prepared Bertrand Louis for the death of his wife, and he wrapped his sorrow and loneliness tightly about himself as his duty to Celine. He could still hear her voice clearly, advising and comforting; but to ease the agony of lying alone in bed, he would empty a small flask of rum that he bought every afternoon on the way home. Soon, the laughing face of the pirate on the bottle's label was more easily recalled than his wife's face.

In their small community, where even words and acts said and done in secrecy were soon known to all, Bertrand's drinking alarmed his pupils' parents. They came to him with hastily assembled and clumsy explanations, and many kind words for him.

'My husband needs the boy to help him in the office. You see?' said one.

'Things are a bit tight for us now; she'll come back when the money is better,' said another.

'We don't want to move the children. I know they won't have a better teacher . . . but the school is so far, and maybe they should try the school nearer home. We will send the younger ones here. You have the best school for the four-year-olds,' said yet another.

'Eh . . . you're doing a good, good job,' they assured him; but the children left. Six months after Celine's death the little school of St. Boniface was empty. His two helpers found jobs at a clothing store owned by two Lebanese brothers, and Bertrand continued to go to his school at nine o'clock every morning and to leave at three o'clock in the afternoon. The large family of which he was a part, and which did not know of conventions such as uncles or aunts or cousins, shared the pain of its hurt member.

Bertrand's older brother, also named Nicholas, came home with Bertrand after High Mass on a Sunday morning and, after their ritual exchange of regrets over the latest small scandals, mentioned that the younger Nicholas had not seen his aunt Marie-Louise for some weeks.

'I was thinking he should come home with me today,' he said tentatively. When Bertrand did not respond, he continued, 'The boy needs a little break.'

That afternoon, Bertrand helped carry his son's belongings to his brother's home.

Again the family considered, and Celine's sister Solange and her husband, Jean Marc, visited to suggest that Lise come to live with them.

'It will give you a little rest, Bertrand,' Jean said.

So Lise moved to a part of the city where the stores began and where one saw new faces every day.

The loss of his family and his school brought a shame that sat so heavily on Bertrand's shoulders, and so bent his gaze, that his eyes no longer met other eyes but sought each little piece of ground where his next step would fall.

One month later, Bertrand Louis sold St. Boniface to a carpenter to be made into a workshop. With the money, he opened separate savings accounts for Nicholas and Lise at Barclays Bank, but did not tell them. It took him only one week more to rent his home with most of its furniture; the rest he gave to his brother and to Jean and Solange Marc. He packed a wooden crate with a small Philips radio, kitchenware and some of Celine's cherished things. His own clothes he put into a cardboard suitcase and, at two o'clock on a Saturday afternoon, he left the capital for Consolation.

A long time ago, when his adolescent concupiscence made these matters memorable, he had overheard a market vendor joke that the women of Consolation were easy and were capable of breaking a man's waist in bed. Bertrand Louis did not crave sexual mischief – Celine's memory was still too near for that – but he supposed that only an easy woman would oblige a plain and failed school teacher.

His shirt, buttoned at the wrists, and his black tie of mourning secured for him a seat at the front of a bus painted in happy shades of brown, green, red and yellow, and named 'Sputnik'. This name was unwittingly quite appropriate as the bus would follow a route which took it climbing towards the sky, then hurtling down precipitous slopes at death-mocking speeds through country where everything clung to hillsides.

When he arrived at Consolation two and half hours later, dirty, hot and cramped, with his stomach a hostile and angry organ, he was advised to find the house of Madame Ferdinand, who could rent him a room. Two boys agreed to carry his suitcase for ten cents, and a small procession set off. For a dozen village children who followed Bertrand Louis, a new face and mysterious baggage were matters of enormous interest and rich entertainment indeed. A few minutes later, Madame Ferdinand found her small front yard filled by an excited delegation of helpers, well-wishers, curiosity-seekers and guides, led by a man who seemed to be trembling with apprehension and embarrassment.

'Come and rest yourself.' said Madame Ferdinand.

In the city, Lise's pleasure at escape from her father's drunkenness and discipline hid for a short time the realities of her new situation. Her aunt Solange fully expected her to pay for her salvation by assuming the roles of nurse to their two-year-old son and of live-in maid. For two years, Solange foiled her attempts to find a salaried job; and for two years, Jean Marc's lust for Lise caused him to suffer like a sixteenth-century Spanish non-believer who was particularly hated by the Inquisition.

At first, Jean Marc poured every kindness on Lise. Then his wife's warning glances kept him at a safe distance, but did not protect him from the perfume of forest water that made his nostrils flare and squeezed the breath from his chest. For two years, he was forced to make a special effort not to call out Lise's name when he made love to his wife. Eventually he eased his torment by pretending it was Lise – not Solange – beneath him in bed.

Solange did not mind when her husband's perfunctory poundings became frenzied, turbulent upheavals. In fact, she enjoyed his breathless and impatient removal of her clothes as this reminded her of her adolescent escapades beneath her parent's house with a boy from the neighbourhood – now her employer. But when Jean began demanding repeats and waking her before morning and wanting to try new positions, she told him firmly that he would get it when and how she decided, or he could go play with his hand.

One Thursday, at noon, Jean Marc asked for two hours off from his job, and hurried home fighting the urge to run. He walked quickly and with a determined frown to discourage conversation from anyone who knew him. He went to the back door that he knew would be unlocked and entered the kitchen, sweating and breathless.

'Who's there?' Lise's voice asked, almost screaming in fear.

'It's OK . . . it's me, 'Jean said, going into the living-room where she sat, her eyes wide with question and apprehension.

'How come you're home so early?' Lise asked.

'Oh, I wasn't feeling too good. I came for some liver salts,' Jean Marc said.

He went to a kitchen cupboard, poured some powder into a glass, added water and quickly drank the effervescing liquid.

'Where's the baby?' he asked.

'Sleeping.'

He walked to the window overlooking the street, glanced about quickly, then moved to her and, taking her by the arm, pulled her towards the bedroom. Then she understood.

'No, please, no, Uncle Jean!' she said, trembling violently. 'Auntie Solange. The baby. Please . . . Please!'

'Look, everything will be all right. You'll like it. I won't hurt you,' he said impatiently.

He pushed her down on the bed, but when he looked at her face, wet with tears and mucus, he wanted to run back to his office in the hope that she would not mention anything to his wife. Then the smell of forest water lifted from the bed and suffocated what was left of his conscience and his self-control. He pushed her skirt up to her chest and abused the girl whose father had beaten her without real cause, whose mother had died prematurely, who had been exploited by her relatives and who had never harmed anyone.

When he was finished, he dressed hurriedly and left after a breathless warning: 'You better not say a word to your Auntie.'

Lise felt the warm trickle down her thigh and knew it was blood. She tried to rise but the pain was too intense. For a moment, she, lay staring at the ceiling, waiting for the burning to pass. Suddenly, the pain receded until it was no more than an unimportant sensation and in its place came a harsh, dispassionate coldness. She did not rise from the bed.

The baby awoke and began crying, but Lise did not move. Four hours later when Solange arrived, Lise listened disinterestedly as she called.

'Lise? Lise? But where's that girl? Oh baby, you're soaked. All right, all right. Lise?'

Solange pushed open the door of the bedroom and her shock was so great that she almost dropped the baby.

'Lise! Lise! Who did that? Lise!' she cried.

The voice that answered was so disconsolate, so frigid and distant that Solange cringed visibly when she heard it.

'Your husband.'

A scream rose from Solange Marc's throat, growing and growing until it was no longer audible but had become a low, relentless throb that shook the furniture and the walls and the house.

Lise pushed herself slowly off the bed and walked past the woman kneeling on the floor, screaming and holding her baby tightly to her breast. It took her five minutes to pack her clothes into the blue suitcase she had arrived with. She reached behind a large chest in a corner of the room, removed a small paper bag furred with grey dust and took out her entire savings – twenty-seven dollars and sixty cents. She stopped briefly in the bathroom to wipe her face and legs, then left the house.

The south-western corner of the city was called The Market, although there was no market there. On Saturday nights, men who did not live in The Market walked slowly along the road which led through the quarter, or drove slowly along the road, searching for the women who had ten minutes of fury to sell.

Lise Louis walked along that road at the time of the evening when darkness was unsure of itself and faces were difficult to discern. She walked a little more quickly when she saw the sweet-vendor with the red and green madras headscarf.

'Ay, it's my little sea-breeze!' the woman called when she recognized Lise. 'You're on your way to America?'

Then she saw the girl's face more clearly and Lise's godmother's smile did not go on to laughter.

The sweet-vendor who knew the faces and secrets of all the parents and the children in The Market, who knew of all quarrels and liaisons, who was an unstoppable source of advice, did not know what to say to her godchild. So she enfolded Lise in large, soft, brown arms that smelled of oranges, coconut oil and Yardley powder.

Two days later Annette Chalon took Lise to see her brother, Guy. He owned a small pharmacy, where he sold painkillers and remedies for ailments that were not yet known at the great universities of Europe and America. He also sold predictions on matters of love and wealth, and, to those who wanted more grace than they had received at Sunday mass, he sold cards containing fragments of the clothes of energetic French and Italian saints. One of his most successful items was a white, perforated plaster, eight inches square, with a black poultice that adhered to the skin with industrial determination. This plaster, when applied to the chest or back and accompanied by appropriate prayers, was known to siphon out the most remote and obstinate thoracic pains.

Guy Chalon did not understand why Lise stayed beyond his embrace. Annette, as if by way of explanation, nudged him. 'We have to talk,' she said.

'Watch the counter, Lise,' Guy said,' if anybody comes, call me.'

The two went into a back room and occasionally Lise would hear her godfather's voice: 'No! . . . Ah no! . . . You think this is something! . . . Ah, ah, ah! . . . No ! . . . What are you telling me!'

When her godparents re-emerged, Guy was trying to be casual about removing an imaginary speck of dirt from the corner of an eye.

'Lise,' he said, 'You want to come help me in the store? Your godmother says you're staying by her.'

Again the family's arms reached out to pull in its own, and the huge pharmacist, whose laughter exploded so deep inside that only the peaks were heard, took in his god-daughter. Lise sat behind the counter with him, waiting for his wife to come home from shopping, staring in fascination at his belly, which resembled a great wave that had jelled while on its way to his knees.

Chapter 3

Two months after his twentieth birthday, Maurice Jacob discovered the meaning of life: the purpose of man's existence was to make God laugh.

On a Wednesday evening in August, the hurricane announced its coming by turning the sky grey and purple, and holding back all the winds so that even the breeze from the Atlantic stopped. At three o'clock on Thursday morning, it arrived as an utterly evil scream that rushed from the ocean and up the valley of St. Pierre. The wind, heavy with rain, hit the houses, tearing off shingles and roofs and twisting and bending trees until their branches surrendered from exhaustion. The storm searched the valley for victims – uprooting trees that had lost their support in the saturated soil, flattening outhouses and livestock pens, blowing away chickens and ducks, and crushing homes with torn trees and with irresistible blasts of wind. The rain came through narrow spaces around doors and windows, and the thatched and shingled roofs served only to guide the water into discrete torrents.

At two o'clock in the afternoon, the winds suddenly dropped and Maurice was ordered to go and relieve himself outside, as his flatulence was beginning to overcome the family's concern with the storm.

The outhouse had disappeared, so Maurice stooped behind two large rocks to hide himself from the house and road. He had almost finished, when the ground shook and a deep sigh of ineffable anguish and regret came from the direction of the house. Then came a roar, a rush of wind and silence. In panic, Maurice pulled on his trousers and rushed towards his home.

There was no house. The clay soil of the hillside, made heavy and slippery by the rain, had shed a strip of the slope, taking his home, his sister Ti-Therese, his father, Marius Tisson, and his mother, Antoinette Jacob. They were now buried under tons of orange clay at the bottom of the hill.

Maurice heard a desolate cry within his mind as though his soul were rushing about asking for escape. Then while his body settled to the ground, his voice – seemingly from a great distance – said in a tone of resignation and irony, 'Life waited until I was shitting to shit on me.'

The family of Serges Jean-Baptiste took in Maurice Jacob without hesitation or consideration.

After a week of mourning, Maurice Jacob refused to wear a black arm-band any longer, saying that the world was so cruel, so beyond reason or understanding, that God must have created man for his amusement. If God wanted a good laugh, then he, Maurice, would oblige. So his sense of mischief, already well developed in his childhood, was reinforced by a new enthusiasm for women, music and work.

When he was nine years old, Maurice Jacob's mother had abandoned all efforts at physical punishment of a son who was as hard as an ebony board. His father's attempts at discipline were usually weakened by amusement at his son's pranks, and eventually he resigned himself to predictions of prison and begging for Maurice.

His foster parents, now under critical scrutiny by the souls of Marius Tisson and Antoinette Jacob, sought the advice of Father Alphonse on ridding the boy of the evil spirit that possessed him. They were convinced that it was a soul lost between heaven and hell that had caused Maurice to summon the village to their home one Sunday to buy what they thought was fish, but had turned out to be two skinned mongooses. That Sunday afternoon while his new parents were at a christening, the doleful call from a conch-shell, signalling the arrival of fish for sale, went through the village, bringing the women out with gourds and small basins and guiding them to the home of Remy Jean-Baptiste. They found there, hanging from a clothes-line, two small, pink, gutted carcasses. Maurice Jacob and his conch-shell were hidden in the branches of a mango tree, where Maurice was offering that act to heaven.

In 1951, Maurice Jacob saw his first motion picture, 'The Three Musketeers.' It had taken the conductor on the six o'clock bus to the capital all of two and a half hours to persuade Maurice Jacob to agree to spend ten cents to see the latest film rage. All of the explanations of the phenomenon had not prepared Maurice for the miracle of noise and colour that burst from the previously white wall before him. During the many breaks, when the bored projectionist changed reels, Maurice Jacob had sat in awed silence. He had not even joined in when jaded patrons voiced their impatience at interruptions and shouted their convictions about the projectionist's sexual perversions and his bestial parentage. For two hours, he sat in wonderment, suspense and terror as magnificent horses galloped over him, and sabres sliced through the air inches from his face.

Maurice Jacob's life was permanently changed. During the next two years, he would attend the ten o'clock Saturday matinee at the Sans Pareil Cinema in the capital once a month. By his third film, his apprehension had disappeared although he had no inkling of how the images had been projected, and he proceeded to give vent to his enthusiasm. Scores of blond, blue-eyed cowboys owed their lives to timely advice shouted by Maurice, and many times he had saved Tarzan when he warned of the approach of black cannibals shouting 'Umgawa!'

Those were good years for Maurice Jacob, muscled as a wrestler and with an appetite for food and women that the people of Consolation pretended not to notice, while using him as a standard for their own doings.

When Maurice Jacob learned that the national boxing champion 'Kid Superb,' whose grandparents had come from the neighbouring village of Two Hills, had been challenged, Maurice's pride threatened to rupture his heart. After Sunday mass he persuaded a group of friends to place bets on their favourite son, and ten dollars was left with Estephan St. Pierre, because Father Alphonse had refused to hold wagered money. The priest had also hesitated to say a blessing for Kid Superb's success, but had promised to pray for the good health of both boxers, with an extra word for their compatriot.

On the day of the match, Consolation Reliable Transport left with twenty-five sports enthusiasts who had never seen a boxing match. More money was bet on Kid Superb with a roving bookmaker who assured them of a fourfold return. Twenty-five countrymen of the Kid sat near the ring and waited for their champion to bring them glory and dollars.

The footwork of Kid Superb may have inspired envy in his opponent for its rapidity and complexity. It did not protect the champion from the hard, accurate blows of an unexciting but methodical technician. Soon after the beginning of the third round, the challenger caught Kid Superb at a moment when The Kid seemed to have missed a step in his wonderful foot movements. The blow came so fast and with such force that it surprised even the challenger. The Kid's head snapped back, and for the next few seconds the world was blinding white and he no longer had a body; but he managed to pull himself up on the ropes before the referee could count him out. For the rest of the match, he scampered about, but before the end of the round, he had decided that he could not win and he did not want to be hit like that again. The Kid suddenly turned away from the challenger, climbed over the ropes and tried to run out of the arena. His supporters from Consolation, believing that their champion had an obligation to their pride and their money, tried to help. Maurice Jacob and two others grabbed the escaping boxer and asked him gently to go back. When he refused, they lifted him and threw him back into the ring. The crowd cheered.

'But friends,' he pleaded, 'I can't go back, the man will kill me.' And he tried to climb out again.

'Look. We put our good money on you, and we . . . we'll kill you if you don't put your backside back in there,' Maurice said. 'Now fight!' And the boxer's friends carried him firmly to the centre of the ring.

The crowd cheered wildly.

Two minutes later, Kid Superb was carried unconscious from the ring. He did not hear any of what would be done to him if he ever set foot in the Valley of St. Pierre.

One Sunday in 1952, Father Alphonse announced that the entire country would be celebrating the twenty-fifth anniversary of the miracle of Fatima – in May, 1927, three children in the village of Fatima in central Portugal had reported a visitation from the Virgin Mary. The priest seemed to shimmer with ecstasy, as one who had been made privy to a great secret of the universe, when he announced that a consecrated statue of the Virgin would be carried in pilgrimage around the country.

'And there will be a stop in Consolation!' he said reverently.

The congregation was so moved that the members almost applauded in church.

When the holy statue with its attendants in dazzling white habits arrived in the capital, the populace immediately went into paroxysms of religious fervor. Innumerable songs of praise, in various states of remembrance, were hurled at Heaven, and rosaries became as common as handkerchiefs. In the boys' schools, truces were declared between warring students, and even severe provocations did not lead to bleeding noses and ripped shirts. In the girls' schools, students walked about with expressions of utmost piety, and gave responses to questions in hushed, breathless voices. There were fewer robberies during that holy week, as thieves hesitated to take anything but essentials such as gold or money; in homes where a statue of the Virgin was displayed, nothing was stolen at all.

Government ministers who had not been to church since their election, attended at least three masses in one week. They walked in, one second before the mass began, preceding their families in solemn procession down the central aisle of the cathedral and sat in the front pews. When they were satisfied that their presence had been noted, they would nod slightly to the priest as if giving their permission for the ceremony to begin.

·It was the happiest week of Father Alphonse's life. He worked so hard that be would forget to eat, and after he fainted from hunger one afternoon, Simone St. Pierre brought him a dinner of braised chicken, rice, macaroni and red beans. She sat nearby to ensure that he ate, and when he had finished, she made him drink a glass of eggnog containing so much brandy that it engraved a fierce smile on his face for the rest of the day.

The great moment arrived. The small, white church had been changed to a red, white and green mound with branches of oleander and hibiscus, and bundles of lilies. Almost every house in the valley was deserted except for the watchdogs that decided to remain silent as there were no people around to annoy with their barking. The adults were dressed in their best and most uncomfortable. All sounds of displeasure were directed at befuddled children fidgeting and scratching in clothes starched to the stiffness of tree bark.

It was a glorious day: the sun grinned, Father Alphonse prayed and the crowd sang. The only unpleasantness of the event was the utterance of a heartfelt sentiment by the saxophonist in the small band, when a grackle flying overhead deposited a black, red and white lump on the right sleeve of his white shirt. Several giggling children received vicarious punishment for the bird's licence.

At seven o'clock in the evening, a convoy of buses, trucks, cars and one motorcycle carried the holy image to the next valley. For two blessed hours Father Alphonse humbly accepted congratulations and assurances that he had had the most successful celebration of the pilgrimage.

It was that success that made it so difficult for Father Alphonse to accept, with any equanimity, the news that an American evangelist would be preaching at Two Hills, only three months after the holy pilgrimage. The priest complained to everyone and so ensured that all of his parishioners would attend the evangelist's revival meeting – although none would have admitted it to him.

Maurice Jacob heard of Father Alphonse's rage when he stopped to talk with Estephan and Simone St. Pierre, on his way home.

'Father Alphonse has been saying words I've only heard from you,' Estephan said, laughing.

'What, he thinks that we are going to leave his church?' Maurice asked.

'It's not that; he thinks the preacher is taking advantage of his big mass last May. Father Alphonse knows the only road to Heaven.' Estephan said.

'Poor devil,' said Simone, 'it was he who told everybody about the revival.'

'I hear he's going to make two infirm people walk . . . the preacher,' said Maurice. 'You're going?'

'Um-hm,' said Simone eagerly.

'Not me,' said Estephan, unable to stretch his dignity to a revivalist's tent.

'I'm going with Madame Ferdinand,' said Simone St. Pierre.

'I think I'll go,' said Maurice after a thoughtful pause.

On the way home, Maurice thought of his parents. Two good people; he had loved them even when he had disobeyed them and laughed at their threats. The church had taken the place of his parents: to be loved but ignored. Now his church was being challenged, and their beloved gadfly, Father Alphonse, was afraid. He stopped at a bamboo grove and selected a section from a dry, fallen trunk.

The evangelist arrived aboard one of two chartered buses from the capital. A tall, imposing American, armed with a nose that rivalled Estephan's and black hair that had been solidified into a helmet by fragrant pomade, he supervised the erection of an open-sided tent, a small stage, kerosene lamps on poles and a public-address system. Two men in wheelchairs were pushed to the front near the stage, and a middle-aged lady who was apparently blind was led to a chair near the two men. Whispers eagerly carried around the crowd word that the preacher would make the two paraplegics walk and heal the lady who was blind, mute and deaf. Some boys immediately left to carry the news through the valley of St. Pierre, and the playground near the school at Two Hills was packed tightly with villagers about to witness miracles to rival those of Fatima.

The evangelist sat on the stage with an open Bible on his knee, smiling at the crowd, and when he thought it was time to start, he nodded at his interpreter and shouted into the microphone.

'People of St. Pierre-uh. I come as a prophet of the Lord-uh. I come to ask you to welcome the Lord-uh into your hearts-uh. Tonight-uh, you will bear witness with me-uh as we celebrate the power of Our Saviour-uh! Amen-uh!'

The interpreter, who had never before heard the cadences of southern American religious sermons, quickly decided to give his impression of what the evangelist had said, and in the French dialect of the villagers said, 'Tonight I will chase away your problems. God has chased away your problems. God has sent me to open your hearts . . .'

So the crowd, suddenly seeing themselves free from all ailments, hurried closer. The evangelist, thus encouraged, began to lose his apprehension about preaching to a crowd of black papists in some unmapped village in a country where few people spoke English.

'Bring to me your sick-uh and infirm-uh and I will make them whole again-uh. Do I hear Amen-uh?'

And the crowd responded enthusiastically, 'Amen-uh!'

The interpreter screamed, 'I will make you rich and happy! Amen-uh!'

After an hour of these happy exchanges, the preacher closed his eyes and bent his head.

'I will now lay my hands upon my afflicted brothers and sisters-uh. And you will see here tonight-uh, the power of Our Saviour make these two walk again, and jump-uh, right before your very eyes-uh. Our sister here, who has never heard the sound of the holy word-uh, who has never seen the Lord's blessed light-uh, who has never sung the Lord's praise-uh, will now be made whole. But before I do these things, brothers and sisters in Christ-uh, let us make a small donation to enable us to continue the Lord's work-uh.'

The interpreter shouted, 'Pass a little money, the man had to pay for gasoline to get here. If you want to see miracles, you will have to help. Alleluia . . . Uh!'

The villagers gave generously; this was cheaper than going to the doctor.

While a tin can was being carried around by the interpreter, the preacher had gone to one of the afflicted and had pushed his chair to the centre of the assembly, under a bright, hissing Coleman lamp.

When collection was over, the evangelist began praying with a rapidity that left the interpreter stranded. He then put his right hand on the paraplegic's head, his left hand on the man's right shoulder and closed his eyes tightly.

'I command you to walk-uh, in the name of the Lord-uh!' he prayed.

At this point, the crowd held rigid by suspense and fear, was assaulted by a loud explosion and a flash of red flame from the rear.

'The Devil! Look out for yourselves!' a voice shouted.

The startled evangelist leaped back, and his three handicapped subjects, suddenly realizing that they were now off anyone's list of priorities, bolted swiftly and unerringly for the nearer bus. The preacher looked at the rapidly disappearing crowd and decided instantly to return to his hotel in the capital. He abandoned his tent, lamp and loudspeakers, and moved with a speed that he had not approached since that Friday night at a brothel in Alabama, when the young seminarian had heard the voice of his hall monitor in an adjoining room shouting, 'Ride baby, ride!'

Estephan St. Pierre heard his wife's helpless laughter as she unlocked the front door. When she came into the light of the lamp, her face was wet with tears and she was blowing her nose into a handkerchief.

'What happened?' Estephan asked, trying to remain serious.

'The devil . . . the devil stopped the meeting. You should have seen the preacher run . . . and his three infirm people,' she said between gales of laughter.

'What devil?'

'Whom do you think?'

'Not Maurice!'

'Naturally,' Simone said. 'The vagabond made a cannon with kerosene and a bamboo tube, and exploded it just when the preacher was about to make a lame man walk. You should have seen how quickly the man healed. He ran faster than the evangelist. And the blind woman . . . she passed them all!'

'What happened to Maurice?' Estephan asked.

'He walked home with me and Madame Ferdinand. He said that when everybody had disappeared, he looked around and decided he didn't want to be alone in the darkness with the real devil, so he ran like hell after the crowd.'

'But what made him do all that?' Estephan asked.

'He said that one mad priest was enough for St. Pierre,' Simone answered.

Six years later, as Father Alphonse lay on his deathbed, he remembered Maurie Jacob, and died during a fit of coughing brought on by uncontrollable laughter.

Chapter 4

The people from the village had come quickly to the bottom of the hill where Maurice Jacob's family was buried by the landslide. They found Maurice standing near two large rocks, holding up his pants with his left hand while the other was stretched out towards the grave of his parents and sister. His face was frozen in horror, and he seemed to be waiting for their hands to push through the earth so that he could help them out. He may have been crying but his face was also wet with the continuing rain. Serges Jean-Baptiste took him gently by the left elbow.

'Come with us, little brother,' he said almost inaudibly.

Maurice walked away slowly with his oldest friend, his gaze still towards the bottom of the hill and his hand still outstretched.

Serges Jean-Baptiste led the crowd of shaken villagers to his house, sharing the turmoil of the others who groped for words and actions to take away a piece of Maurice's grief, and not let him suffer alone. Serges's prayers, said aloud but made incoherent by his crying, were beseeching heaven to let him live long enough to ensure that his friend-brother would live well and die peacefully.

In her small kitchen, Baby Jean-Baptiste stripped Maurice naked and towelled dry the shivering body, made grey and wrinkled by the cold and rain. She then rubbed his chest and back with a white liniment reeking of menthol and eucalyptus oil. Serges gave him a change of clothes, and no one seemed to notice how the ill-fitting clothes made Maurice look even more pathetic.

They did not eat; they could not eat. The house was filled with neighbours who came to give and share and pray. They talked in whispers through the night and into the morning, and the same things were said over and over, but by different voices. Serges would not leave Maurice's side and his thoughts wrestled for something right to say to his friend. He could not say that he was sorry, as the landslide had robbed him of people who were as close to him as his own parents. He could not say that these things would pass: the loss would always lie there, hard, sharp and cruel, even when buried by time and wrinkled memories. When they were both too exhausted to stay awake any longer, Serges spoke to Maurice for the first time since they had come in. He pointed to the palliasse of rags that served as his bed in a corner of a large bedroom he shared with six other siblings.

'There's room for you here . . . which side do you want?' he asked.

Maurice nodded slightly and curled up on the bed, close to the wall, and relived his agony during and between the nightmares.

For the rest of his life, Serges Jean-Baptiste was brother, friend and confessor to Maurice Jacob: the tall, awkward and shy guardian, and his boisterous, laughing and massive ward.

Serge's second passion in life was Ti-Louise Benoit, the most beautiful girl in the valley of St. Pierre. Ti-Louise possessed the beauty that pulls the breath from a man's chest. The small imperfections of her face were put together in a fashion that made boys wish to be men, and caused men to resent their wives and mistresses. She used her beauty as a machete to cut her way through life, leaving many men – suitors, strangers and cousins – bleeding and heartbroken but unregretful. Her mother, Clementine, found Ti-Louise's flirting dangerous and sinful; but her handsome father, Paul Benoit, took pride in his daughter's beauty and boasted that she had inherited it from him. Ti-Louise was not ready for love, even at seventeen, with Serges Jean-Baptiste or with any pursuer in Consolation or Two Hills – until the new extension officer arrived at St. Pierre astride a black, shining, throbbing motorcycle.

The Department of Agriculture had dispatched this young expert, with the mien of a buccaneer, to tell the villagers what they already knew about terracing the hillsides. He would ride his great iron steed, which bore the emblem of crossed rifles of the Birmingham Small Arms factory, along tracks that confounded horses and donkeys, and in his first week had ridden over innumerable pumpkin and sweet-potato vines. The children worshipped him and quickly named their hero, 'Master BSA'.

The men envied and admired him and the younger women lusted quickly and quietly after him. The old women, safe behind the barrier of their years, suggested that he make use of the generous space in their small homes.

Peter Donelly loved them all: the sea, the valley, the people and the wind that blew constantly from the Atlantic. He rented a room in a house near Paul Benoit and his family, where he slept from Mondays to Thursdays. On Friday evenings he returned to his wife and two children in the nearby town of Colline.

Ti-Louise suggested that he eat his meals with her family; so he did. Then she washed and ironed his shirts. Soon Peter Donelly would pray for evening, when he could sit on the steps of Paul Benoit's house to look at the ocean, and steal glances and wink at Ti-Louise. Peter Donelly fell in love with Ti-Louise, at first gently and carelessly, then fiercely and wretchedly. He spent more time weaving fantasies of her than remembering formulations for nitrates and phosphates. Angles and elevations were displaced by obsessions with her body and her walk and her face. On Friday nights he rode back home with the enthusiasm of an adulterer on his way to a stoning.

The two lovers were not able to spend much time together alone. Clementine Benoit had the eyes of a chicken hawk and the ears of a hunting dog. She had been swept off her feet by Paul nineteen years ago and she remembered every trick he had used and every word he had whispered in her willing ear. Behind her kindness to Peter Donelly, and her smiles, was the unspoken warning: 'Don't touch my daughter.'

The monster that haunted those afflicted by unfulfilled love harried Ti-Louise mercilessly. It brought others to the lovers' hastily arranged trysting places, and it alerted Clementine Benoit when Peter Donelly was standing too close, or had spoken too long, to her daughter. So 'Master BSA' completed his two-year tour of duty without touching Ti-Louise except for a quick kiss on a cheek, as he handed her an envelope containing five dollars, on her last birthday.

Six months later, Peter returned on a Saturday morning to see his old friends in Consolation, and to buy some beef in the country – as he had told his wife. The news of his return went through the village as quickly as a secret. Even Serges Jean-Baptiste subdued his jealousy enough to come by the Benoits' home.

'It's you?' they asked.

'Yes,' Peter Donelly said, 'I'm here.'

'And your wife, she's well?'

'Yes.'

'And your children, they're well?'

'Yes.'

'How long are you staying with us this time?'

'A little while.'

'You haven't arrived and you're leaving already?'

'I have to go back soon. I just passed to say hello.'

'Ah-ah, but that's not enough.'

'I know. I'll have to come back more often.'

'Of course, of course,' they said in chorus, nodding.

Peter Donelly shared with them the flask of fragrant white rum that celebrated his return, and chased it down with rain-water from the tall earthenware jar in Clementine Benoit's kitchen.

The joy of seeing their friend from the capital, and the relaxation brought by the rum, overcame Clementine's caution. When Peter suggested that he take Ti-Louise for a short ride, she agreed immediately, thinking it would be amusing to see her daughter screaming in fright on the back of the roaring machine. Peter Donelly could not believe his luck. He mounted the motorcycle and kicked the engine on. Ti-Louise climbed aboard with the whispered help of Peter and an infinitude of instructions, advice and cautions from the bystanders. The BSA growled away, followed by the silent wish of most of those left behind that perhaps Peter Donelly could be persuaded to give each of them a short ride.

Peter headed immediately for the dirt track that led to Great Hole.

'Hold tight,' he said as the motorcycle bounced from rut to rock. The frightened and excited girl followed his instructions with a force that impeded his breathing, but the aroused man would not have noticed if she had fractured several of his ribs. He took her to the low cliffs on the south side of the bay, where yellow daisy-like flowers grew, and into a small, dense copse of *porier* trees and pandanus palms. It took them two minutes, on a bed of dry palm leaves, to satiate the hot sharp-edged urge that had mocked them for two years. She had had the presence of mind to remove her dress, but he had been too impatient and his pants were streaked with moss and soil. He convinced himself that no one would notice the dirt on his knees or the look of guilt and relief on his face.

Clementine Benoit was waiting grim-faced when they returned after forty-five minutes. Her eyes examined their faces and clothes carefully, but she said nothing and entered the house without returning Peter Donelly's smile.

Paul Benoit was sitting on the bench-like step of his house making baby-talk with his youngest child. He grinned at Ti-Louise's unsteadiness when she got off the motorcycle.

'You want one for Christmas?' he asked her.

'Um-um,' she said shaking her head. 'That thing's too dangerous.'

Peter took one of her brothers for a ride; that time he was away for ten minutes; then he said his goodbyes.

Clementine was too busy inside to see him off. He rode home, his accomplishment marred by the thought that pursued him all the way home, shouting: 'She knows . . . she knows!'

Three months later, at their January staff meeting, Peter's replacement at St. Pierre, the one they called 'Zorro' because of his black hats and shirts, beckoned to Peter during a break.

'I hear you've plugged Paul Benoit's daughter,' he whispered.

'Oh shit . . . Oh holy shit!' said Peter Donelly, trying not to fall into the dark, roaring emptiness that had suddenly opened before him.

'You're sure, you're sure it's me?'

'Eh! Christ man, that girl would not have let anyone else touch her . . . from what I hear,' said Zorro.

'What the hell am I going to do? Just once, and the damn girl gets pregnant. Just once, man.'

'The next time you take it out, put it where it belongs,' Zorro said and went back to his seat. Later he said to Peter, 'Go and see the girl and talk to Paul Benoit. I don't think you'll want to talk to Clementine.'

The following Saturday, Peter Donelly came again to Consolation to buy meat. He stopped first at Simone St. Pierre's store to get a sense of the reception he could expect from Paul Benoit. He was unable to broach the subject and Simone did nothing to help; she seemed oblivious to the agitation of a man who would have speeded the coming of his own death. On his way out, Estephan walked with him to the BSA.

'Watch how you walk,' he said with a sad, little smile. 'Don't stub your toe. Carry yourself well.'

'Yes, and you too, Mr. St. Pierre,' said a thoroughly alarmed Peter Donelly.

The sound of his machine had brought out the Benoit family. Paul was sitting on the step and Ti-Louise was standing in the doorway. Her pregnancy was not yet evident and she seemed even more beautiful, despite her expression of concern.

'Mr. Benoit, Ti-Louise,' Peter said.

'Good morning, Mr. Donelly,' said Paul Benoit – not 'Peter,' nor 'Master BSA'.

'Mr Benoit, I came to talk about Ti-Louise.'

'And what are you going to do for my daughter?'

'I have an obligation, Mr. Benoit,' Peter answered. 'I'm going to take care of my obligation.'

'You're married, Mr. Donelly, how are you going to take of my daughter . . .' He paused. 'Ti-Louise, you and the children, get inside.'

'I'll do everything I can, Mr. Benoit. I'll take care of my child,' said Peter.

'Yes, Mr. Donelly, you will take care of your child. Ti-Louise was old enough to know what she was doing. She will have to learn to take care of herself now. If we don't hear from you again, Mr. Donelly, I myself will bring the baby to your home – to your wife. Good, that is all I have to say.'

The next day, Peter Donelly withdrew fifty dollars from his savings account at his credit union. If his wife found out, he would explain that it was for repairs to his motorcycle. He mailed the money to Ti-Louise, in care of her father, with a brief note asking that she let him know if she needed anything.

For two years, Serges Jean-Baptiste had suffered impotently, as the city man had ridden his shiny black machine all over his dreams. And to find out that, even after leaving Consolation, Peter Donelly had inflicted the worst of all possible mortifications on the woman that Serges loved! He was wretched beyond respite. His unhappiness was so profound, and so unmistakable, that even Maurice Jacob would not tease him about it.

For two more years, Serges Jean-Baptiste watched as

Ti-Louise's baby daughter moved from sucking her mother's breast to clutching her skirt. His feelings towards Ti-Louise had stiffened but had not hardened into hate. The country people knew each other so intimately and needed each other so frequently that, although they occasionally disguised their love with jealousy or disappointment or pride, the love was always near, eagerly awaiting the call of need or weariness. Feeding her baby had diminished the impertinence of Ti-Louise's breasts, but she remained a beautiful woman, and Maurice Jacob finally decided it was time that Serges regained his interest or he himself would yield to temptation. One afternoon, he returned home with some peeled sticks of sugar-cane and a ripe papaya.

'I'm bringing these for Ti-Louise's baby. Come with me,' he said to Serges.

'How's the baby going to eat the cane?' Serges asked, trying to hide his agitation over having to talk to Ti-Louise again.

'Well she can eat the papaya. You and Ti-Louise can eat the cane.

'I don't think so, Maurice. I have things to do. Next time,' Serges said.

'Look, stop that . . . bring a bottle of honey and move yourself.'

Serges left with him after washing his face, neck and arms very carefully and putting on a clean shirt. He also selected a quart of logwood-flower honey.

When they arrived at Paul Benoit's house, Maurice shouted, 'Benoit! Where's my baby. I've come for her.'

Paul Benoit came outside followed by Clementine, who was carrying their granddaughter.

'Look at me, Maurice. If you insist that one of my dog's pups is yours, you're welcome to search in the yard for it,' Paul said, laughing.

'Ay then, let's ask Ti-Louise. Ti-Louise!' he called.

Her voice came from the kitchen: 'Maurice Jacob. What do you want?'

'My baby.'

She came outside. 'How are you, Maurice? How are you, Serges?' she said in greeting.

'Suffering,' answered Maurice.

'Managing,' said Serges. 'We brought some little things for the baby.'

'Well, it's about time, Serges,' said Ti-Louise, 'You've been neglecting your baby.'

Serges Jean-Baptiste did not hear the others laughing at his obvious embarrassment. He was utterly and hopelessly in love with Ti-Louise again. For the next eight months, he would stop at Paul Benoit's home whenever he could find some excuse, and he plied Ti-Louise with so much honey that Clementine soon found it unnecessary to buy sugar.

In the following weeks, Serges Jean-Baptiste heard very good reasons from Maurice, aided by Estephan and Simone St. Pierre, for marrying Ti-Louise. For these eight months, Serges gave them equally good reasons for fearing rejection – it was too soon, Donelly might come back, Ti-Louise probably regarded him as a brother, she possibly hated men now, and so on. A snake settled the matter for Serges Jean-Baptiste and Ti-Louise Benoit.

Serges was walking with Estephan St. Pierre after Sunday mass when he said, 'Estephan, you know the bees' nest in the mahogany tree on your place in the hills?'

'Yes?'

'It's still there?'

'Of course, I'm not going to touch it.'

'Can I come and check it on Wednesday morning?'

'Um-hm, I'll come with you,' Estephan said.

That Wednesday morning, Serges brought a protective covering for his head, bellows for smoking out the hive, and some other apparatus that established his authority over bees.

When they had rested from a two-hour climb into the high forest, where the clouds remained until midmorning, Serges removed his sandals and climbed the mahogany tree, carrying a long thin rope. He lowered the rope when he came to the nest, and Estephan attached the equipment Serges requested. Estephan moved to where he hoped he was out of sight of the bees but within earshot of Serges. Fifteen minutes later Serges called out that he was lowering a basket with the combs. Then came his equipment and the rope, and Serges began the climb down. Estephan was some distance from the base of the tree, calling the bees' attention to himself with a small branch that he had meant to chase the insects away with.

In those hills lived a pit-viper that the people called the *fer-de-lance,* the spearhead. It hunted at night for small birds and animals. During the day, it slept under rocks, in holes or among tree roots. It was not an aggressive snake but it would defend itself when threatened. Many times the threat was unintended, as the snakes' colouration made it difficult to see on the leaf-covered forest floor.

Serges Jean-Baptiste jumped down when he was about five feet from the ground, and knew instantly what the hard, slippery body was that moved under his feet. The snake's head flashed back instinctively and its wide-open jaw closed about Serge's right foot. Its two upper fangs bit into the upper part of the foot, then the snake withdrew, leaving one fang broken against a bone, and hanging incongruously from the skin.

Estephan had seen the leaves erupt at Serge's feet and had seen the rapid strike of the *fer-de-lance.* He was already running towards his friend with a machete before the snake released its hold, and he severed its head before it could escape. He quickly pulled the broken fang from one of two small punctures on Serges foot that were beginning to bleed freely.

'Estephan,' said the terrified man, 'I didn't see it. You think I can make it back?'

'It didn't go in too deep . . . it hit the bone. I'm going

to try and suck some of the poison out. Turn your head,' said Estephan.

He poured some drinking water over the foot, and with a pocket knife made two small cross-shaped incisions over each wound. He used a length of rope to tie a tourniquet above the ankle, then sucked at the wounds for a minute – until the pain came. Serges screamed as he felt his foot burst into flame and the fire climb his leg to his groin.

'We have to get to the clinic,' Estephan said. 'Come, I'll help you.'

'I can't walk, Estephan,' said the shocked man.

'Put your right arm around my shoulder. Let's go.'

The two men moved off, sliding down slopes of mud and crawling up interminable hillsides. When they were two miles from the village, Serges collapsed.

'Leave me here,' he said to Estephan. 'Get to the clinic . . . get a horse . . . I'll be OK.'

Estephan St. Pierre considered this for a few seconds, then decided.

'I'm going to carry you.'

'I'm too heavy, Estephan.'

'I'm going to carry you,' Estephan said with finality.

He helped Serges to climb onto his back and walked slowly, not seeing the inclines or the rocks or the mud, just forcing one foot more, then another. Estephan's breaths came and went like hoarse screams, and his chest burned as if an invisible hand sought to rip his lungs out through his open mouth.

A child who saw them alerted his parents, and soon Serges had been helped off Estephan's back and was rushed off on a horse to the clinic. Estephan collapsed in the grass at the side of the road, and the villagers stood around silently waiting for the thunder of his breathing to quieten. They brought him water and helped him to another horse, then followed him to the clinic.

Serges Jean-Baptiste was fortunate; the fangs had not

penetrated deeply into his foot and most of the snake's venom had been released outside the wounds. He stayed only one week at the hospital. The nurses were sorry to see him go: they would miss the visits by Maurice Jacob, who courted them all, brought them fruits, accidentally brushed against them and told each one that she was God's and his favourite nurse.

Ti-Louise came to visit early on the morning of his second day in the hospital. She sat very close, in the visitor's chair, chasing away flies and fanning his face. She didn't say very much after he had reassured her for the seventh time that he would recover fully. When she left in the afternoon to catch the two o'clock bus home, Serges had resolved to ask Ti-Louise to marry him.

Half an hour after his return to Consolation, Ti-Louise was at Serges's home to ask what she could do to help. Miriam Jean-Baptiste did not even think of defending her son, when Ti-Louise sat determinedly on the bed covered with a fresh white sheet printed with pink and red lilies of an unknown species.

As soon as his mother left, Serges withstood only one assault from Ti-Louise's smile. He asked in a tone meant to suggest that he had pondered the question for many years, 'When are you going to get married?'

'When are you going to ask me?' she answered.

'Me?' he asked in great amazement. 'You'd marry me?'

'Um-hm,' Ti-Louise said.

'What?'

'Um-hm,' She repeated.

'What is this?' Serges asked in exasperation. 'I keep asking you to marry me and you keep saying, "Um-hm, Um-hm". If you mean "Yes," then say "Yes",' Serges concluded with an assertiveness that befitted a man from Consolation, but one that Ti-Louise would never permit him again.

'Yes,' she said, 'but what about my baby . . . Nadiege?'

'So, I'll have the most beautiful baby in St. Pierre,' said Serges Jean-Baptiste with a shrug.

'You'll have to work this out with my father,' Ti-Louise said in mock seriousness.

Paul Benoit was so smitten by the granddaughter who had inherited her mother's – and her grandfather's – looks, that he scarcely noticed when the money stopped coming from Peter Donelly. He eventually agreed, after many intricate arguments against it, to let the baby live with Ti-Louise and Serges Jean-Baptiste on the understanding that it was a temporary arrangement – a loan, he insisted.

When Peter Donelly learned that Ti-Louise had married, he rode his motorcycle to a deserted place near the bay at Colline, where he cried like an abandoned baby for two hours.

Chapter 5

In December and January, when the mornings were cool enough to require a thin blanket or an extra sheet, Simone St. Pierre would move in her sleep, closer to her husband's warmth. That was the border of their intimacy. During the first two years of their marriage, she had let Estephan clamber over her whenever he wished, as she believed that was her obligation. Simone played no active part in their lovemaking, and never initiated the act, which she saw as a sequence of inconveniences that were not worth the wait for an occasional flash of pleasure. The transformation of the tall, handsome man with the burning eyes, into a blind, grunting, rank shape at night, disappointed her; but she was unable to intimate that to Estephan St. Pierre, whose pride was as sharp and brittle as a splinter of the volcanic bombs that littered their valley. She said nothing. She was a good wife.

Estephan St. Pierre approved of his wife's unresponsiveness in bed during their first month of marriage. He had not expected a virgin to be expert in those matters, and he would teach her in time. But Simone never became the lunging, screaming, insatiable partner he secretly wanted. It was not proper for a man to say certain things to his wife – maybe to his mistress – and Simone was probably unsure that pleasure should be given and taken from an act so closely related to mortal sin. Estephan suffered silently. He could not express troubles like these to his wife or priest or friends.

His disappointment turned into resentment, and sometimes when he awoke at night and found her arm across him, he denied himself even that small pleasure by gently lifting her arm off, or slowly rolling away. Except in December and January, when he found her warmth comforting. His resentment turned to anger when he learned of his infertility: anger against himself, his childhood disease, fate, his parents, and the wife who knew of his infirmity. The torments crowded into his thoughts at night, in the wide darkness when his eyes would find nothing to examine, and would return to his mind, to discover new doubts and uncertainties. Their lovemaking became infrequent, then stopped. Sometimes he would awake fully aroused, and roll over to Simone and fumble with her clothes, until she mumbled, 'Umm . . . I'm sleeping.'

Then a cold flood would wash away his tumescence and he would force his thoughts to things that he had to do for the day, and allow once more the frightening and daring thought of taking a mistress.

Again and again, Estephan struggled for the right word or the right touch that would hint at his want to Simone. And Simone, believing that Estephan had lost interest in her, would smile indulgently when he suggested, 'Let's sleep naked tonight.'

'Since when did you begin getting younger?' she would ask.

On Easter Sunday, Simone's parents came to visit. Christopher Napoleon La Forêt methodically set about drying the inside of a bottle of Estephan's brandy. Estephan followed dutifully, and was happily drunk when Laure La Forêt pulled Christopher aboard the evening bus to Two Hills. Two glasses of anisette had relaxed Simone's inhibitions, and she found herself becoming excited by Estephan's lewd suggestions, and by his naked body as she helped him undress. She got quickly into bed and waited for him, but the brandy rebuffed his intent – after three attempts, he surrendered in flaccid defeat and confusion.

Simone ignored her own discomfort and rubbed his shoulder.

'It's OK . . . it's OK,' she kept saying softly, but Estephan moved to the edge of the bed, out of reach.

The next day, Estephan collected the remnants of his dignity, and defied a searing headache sufficiently, to go down to the bay to mend the seine he shared with five other villagers. His headache ebbed so imperceptibly that he did not notice when it stopped. He allowed his mind to wander away from his work when his fingers no longer needed his attention, and to wonder whether he had suffered the ultimate abasement of losing his manhood. The thought besieged him until it was time to leave, and on the way home he sought refuge behind the resolve to prove himself with another woman.

The opportunity came, even when Estephan did not expect it, because his intent had opened the door. The schoolmaster's son had decided to have his wedding in Consolation, where he was a more important person than in the capital where he lived and was only a store clerk. The villagers would not have cared; the festivities were an opportunity to listen to the speech of the city folk and to discuss their clothes. During a break in the dancing (while the musicians were making up for the deprivations of the last hour, and ignoring the shouts of Maurice Jacob who had been calling on them to 'Give it gas . . . give it gas!'), Maurice came to Estephan Jacob and pulled him outside. '*Compère,*' he said, struggling to subdue his loud whisper, 'Did you see the two women I've been dancing with?'

'Yes. Why?'

'Well, a little while ago, I went to the back with one . . . there's a small shed there . . . I watered her little garden until I was dry. And now her friend is asking about you. What do you think?' Maurice said.

'Maurice! you're crazy!' Estephan said, almost breathless from the jolt his conscience had received.

'Look friend, enjoy yourself . . . who'll ever know?' Maurice said. He was beginning to feel like something dirty lying in Estephan's path.

'Maurice, Simone's here; how can I do that?' Estephan asked, but Maurice had sensed his wavering.

'Just excuse yourself for a minute . . . I'll look out for

you . . . and I'll tell the woman. Let me know when you're ready.'

Estephan went back inside talking loudly, surprised that no one noticed the agitation that he felt blazing from his face. He listened quietly to friends who came to talk, nodded when he thought it was appropriate, then excused himself to smoke a cigarette.

Maurice was waiting outside. 'Ay! So tonight you're going to light a little fire?' he joked.

Estephan did not want to joke; he wanted to go to the toilet – his stomach writhed with fear and anticipation. 'I don't think that's going to work, Maurice.'

'Listen, the woman is waiting for you. You want me to go and tell her Estephan St. Pierre is afraid?' Maurice asked.

'It's not that . . . I'm not ready,' Estephan said.

'You think you'll ever get a chance like this again?' Maurice asked. 'Listen, *Compère,* I wouldn't do this for anybody else. Go on, enjoy yourself.'

He took Estephan by the elbow and guided him to a small shed that smelt of copra and burnt wood.

'Ay,' he said softly into the dark doorway, 'my friend's here.'

'Good,' a woman's voice said. Estephan entered and walked carefully, searching with his feet for obstacles, towards the voice that said, 'Here, I'm here.' He bent down when he could hear her breathing and reached out to touch a bed of empty jute sacks. He felt around and touched a bare thigh.

'Quick!' the voice said again. Estephan dropped his trousers and underpants and crawled on his hands and knees over the woman, who had pulled her dress up and who was naked from her waist down.

'You're ready?' he asked.

'Yes . . . yes!' she said impatiently.

He lowered himself, drowning out the last plaintive calls of his conscience with the clangour of his heart and breathing that were shouts of triumph. He braced himself with arguments that he had to prove himself and that Simone had forced him to this. When his thighs lay between the woman's, she groaned with pleasure and at that instant his body convulsed, and his exultation was snatched and discarded in a stream that poured over the woman's belly. Then he collapsed upon her.

'What happened?' she asked.

'I came . . . I didn't . . .' he said, searching for explanation.

'Get off me,' she said impatiently. 'Do you have a kerchief?'

He stood up and put his clothes on quickly. He was glad that the darkness hid his confusion and shame.

'Here,' said the woman, and he felt in the darkness for her hand, and took his sodden handkerchief.

'You better go,' she said again, and Estephan passed through the dimly lit, low doorway and forced himself to walk calmly towards the house, while his mind searched frantically for some fragment of comfort from an evening of disaster.

Maurice Jacob was waiting near the house, grinning.

'Come on, come on, tell me, how was it?' he asked. 'How was the woman?'

'Nothing happened,' said Estephan. He could not think of a convincing lie and Maurice would hear the truth anyway.

'What do you mean, "nothing happened" . . . she changed her mind?'

'It wasn't the woman . . . it was me . . . I finished before I started.'

'Oh-oh,' Maurice said, sorrowing for his friend. 'That's all right, we can arrange something for another time . . . when you're more relaxed. I know another woman . . .'

'Maurice,' said Estephan, 'I don't think I want to talk about women now.'

And perversity, having again tripped Estephan, tightened its grip on his spirit and waited for opportunities.

Four days after the Prime Minister called for new elections, a representative of the government party, the Peoples' Alliance for Progress, visited Estephan St. Pierre. Estephan watched with mild disgust as the small, fat man, glistening with the contentment of one who has been well rewarded for lying and stealing, rolled up the short path to Simone's store. Estephan hoped that the visit would not ruin his Sunday.

'Morning, morning everybody. Mr. St. Pierre, Madame St. Pierre . . . It's along time . . . how are you. Eh?'

'Not too bad,' said Simone.

'Managing,' said Estephan.

'Well . . . well. Good . . . good . . ,' Lenox Marchand said, settling himself on a bench by the door.

'Water?' asked Simone, and left to get a glass before Lenox Marchand could reply.

'How are the crops, eh, Mr. St. Pierre?' Lenox Marchand asked, with profound interest.

'Same as always, Mr. Marchand. And when we don't get rain, we have to rely on the sea.'

'. . . on the sea,' Lenox echoed sympathetically.

'The village is growing . . .'

Estephan continued, 'We keep hearing that the government will help us get water to Consolation . . .'

'Of course, of course, Mr. St. Pierre,' the party man said. 'That's why I'm here. We want to know what you want, what we can do. It's our government, Mr. St. Pierre, not mine!'

Estephan St. Pierre laughed. 'And you'll tell us the same thing next election, Mr. Marchand.'

'Ah, no, Mr. St. Pierre! Thank you Madame Simone,' Lenox Marchand said, drinking gratefully from the glass that Simone handed him.

'We have so many things to do, every village wants something important . . .' Lenox Marchand paused to brush away the village flies that had come in great numbers to welcome a new source of sweat. 'But we have to win the elections first.'

'And you want me to help?' asked Estephan.

'Well, you have a lot of influence in the valley,

Mr. Estephan,' said Lenox Marchand, hoping that he sounded sufficiently sincere.

'How am I going to do that?' asked Estephan.

'Mr. St. Pierre!' the party agent said in astonishment. 'People rely on you for advice. They respect you and Madame Simone. You don't have to campaign for us, just welcome our candidate, put in a little word for us . . . nothing big . . . not too much of your time.'

'And if your party wins the election, you'll help us get water in the valley?'

'Ay! But of course, of course. I myself will make it my duty to see that the Water Works people start on that.'

'Uh-huh,' Estephan said softly.

'Madame Simone,' Lenox Marchand said, 'you're laughing; you don't believe I'm serious?'

'Mr Marchand,' Simone said, 'every five years somebody comes from the capital . . .'

'. . . comes from the capital,' said Lenox Marchand.

'. . . and tells us that if we help them win the elections, they will fix the roads, put in water, build a new school . . .'

'. . . build a new school,' Lenox repeated, his brow creased in concern.

'And after the elections, the good-for-nothings stick their backsides in the city and forget the country people.'

'. . . forget the country people,' Lenox Marchand said, his face saddened by the perfidy of politicians who would neglect their constituents. He shook his head mournfully at what he had just learned from Simone.

'Not this time, Madame St. Pierre,' he said, 'You have my word. I'll tell you this thing: Lenox Marchand will look after Consolation.'

'And Two Hills,' said Simone.

'And, of course, Two Hills.'

They gave him water from a green coconut to drink and watched as his throat jumped for joy at his easy triumph.

Later, as Lenox drove away in his shiny red Vauxhall, Estephan said to the departing car, 'You don't give them enough and they ignore you; you give them too much and they walk all over you . . . just like a woman.'

'What are you talking about?' Simone asked.

'Nothing . . . nothing,' Estephan said as he went to repair the thatched roof of the cassava shed.

On the following Friday evening, a young, well-dressed man came to the store.

'Madame St. Pierre, good night,' he said.

Simone looked at the familiar face in the lamplight, then cried in delight, 'Alexis! Ti-Alexis! But you're not Ti-Alexis any longer. Look at you . . . come kiss me.' She hugged her old schoolmate and neighbour from Two Hills.

'But how are you? Well?'

'Yes,' he answered.

'And the family?'

'Everybody's well.'

'They're all well?'

'Yes.'

'I haven't seen you for so long, you're in the city now?' she asked.

'Yes.'

'And you like it?'

'I miss St. Pierre,' he said politely.

'I know . . . it's so hot and crowded in the city,' she said, and as the ritual of greeting was over, she called out to Estephan, 'Estephan, you'd never guess who's here . . . it's Alexis Daumas.'

After the two men had shaken hands and embraced, Simone went to get a bottle of anisette.

'You've forgotten us, Alexis,' Estephan said.

'I've been so busy with a little business in the city, Mr. Estephan; I have a small car-repair place.'

'And what brought you here tonight . . . that's your car?'

'Yes,' Alexis replied. 'Well, Mr. Estephan, I'm thinking of running for this district in the next elections.'

Estephan looked at him in astonishment. 'You mean you've joined the New Workers' Party?'

'Yes,' Alexis replied proudly. 'We're all young, hard working and honest . . .'

'Yes,' said Estephan with resignation, 'and you will clean up everything and provide a better future for all of us.'

'Give us a chance, Mr. Estephan.' Alexis said, smiling self-consciously.

'Look Alexis . . . last Sunday, a man from the Progress Party was here. He asked for my support. I said I would help,' Estephan said.

'But Mr. Estephan, you know these people only want to hear from us on voting day. They'll never do anything for Consolation or Two Hills,' Alexis Daumas said, trying to suppress the feeling that Estephan St. Pierre had betrayed them all, had sold out his people to thieves and liars. He took a deep breath, and looked out into the darkness for a few seconds. Simone had come back with a tray on which stood three small glasses.

'Thank you, Madame Simone,' said Alexis taking a glass.

The three friends clinked their glasses and Alexis spoke of Frederick Albin, whom he had visited occasionally at the psychiatric hospital.

'You know,' he said, 'Frederick is the smartest man I have ever spoken with . . . the man knows everything. He reads about two books a day.'

'We wanted to visit him,' said Simone St. Pierre, 'but they told us he didn't want any visitors.'

'I know. I have a friend there, a male nurse. He persuaded Frederick to let me come and see him.'

'How does he look?' asked Estephan.

'Pale and thin. I don't know what people here will do when he gets out. He should come back to Consolation,' Alexis answered.

Estephan and Simone nodded. 'This is his home,' Estephan said.

'Well, Mr. Estephan,' said Alexis, 'what to do now?'

'I don't know what to tell you, Little Brother. It would be good for you to win, but I don't know for you. You will go and tell people the truth and they will take you for a fool. I don't know what could make you want to join that band of executioners in the capital. Maybe I shouldn't try to discourage you, Ti-Alexis, but you know how it is,' Estephan said.

'So you can't help, *Compère*?' asked Alexis.

'Give me some time . . . let me think about it,' Estephan said.

They embraced, and Simone saw him off with a small bag of vegetables and fruits.

'Carry yourself well,' they called.

'Yes. God will bless you,' he replied, and drove away.

'What are you going to do now?' Simone asked.

'I don't know . . . I'm going to sleep. Piss and misery on all politicians,' he answered, and went out into the darkness, swearing.

The ruling party's candidate for the electoral district that included the valley of St. Pierre was a thin, timid landowner from the neighbouring valley of Palmiers. The Honourable Victorin Raphael Delaire had had no interest in politics – and had never voted – until the Prime Minister visited him at home and asked him to represent the district. Victorin Delaire wished he had had the courage to refuse, but was routed by the Prime Minister's frown, Lenox Marchand's leer, and his wife's open-mouthed astonishment. Dorcas Delaire did not permit her husband to consider declining the offer of simultaneous canonization and coronation; and Victorin Delaire was to spend most of the next five years as a special assistant to the Prime Minister, sitting in an uncomfortable chair in the Legislative Council, worrying about his wife, his crops and his ignorance of parliamentary language and procedures. The only pleasure he received from the whole affair was the privilege of being allowed to view parades in their entirety.

The election campaign arrived in Consolation in a discordance of whistles and screams that came from two loudspeakers mounted on Lenox Marchand's Vauxhall. Victorin Delaire sat in the passenger seat, waving tentatively to villagers along the road; they stood paralyzed by the noise, and did not recognize their candidate. The car and clamour stopped at Estephan St. Pierre's home, and Victorin Delaire got out and went to greet his host.

'Mr Delaire, good afternoon. How are you?' said Estephan in a voice that reminded the legislator of the bass drum in the police band.

'Mr. St. Pierre . . . Mr. St. Pierre,' said Victorin Delaire anxiously, 'you look so well . . . yes, yes. How is Madame Simone?'

'Thanks be to God, very well,' Estephan replied; and the men went into the house.

After they had been served brandy and coconut-water by Simone, Lenox Marchand cleared his throat importantly, wiped his face with a large, madras handkerchief and moved to the edge of his seat, to signify the delicacy of the matter he was about to discuss.

'Mr. St. Pierre,' he said, smiling sadly, 'I see we are going to have an opponent in Mr. Alexis Daumas. Yes?'

'I think so,' said Estephan.

'Good, good. Now, Mr. St. Pierre, I heard that Mr. Daumas is expecting you to support him . . .'

'I haven't promised anything,' Estephan replied.

'I know, I know, but Mr. Daumas is a bright, young man without the experience of Mr. Delaire, and you have already promised your support to Mr. Delaire,' Lenox Marchand continued. 'You see our position, Mr. Estephan? We have to be sure where we stand with you.'

'I promised to introduce Mr. Delaire when he begins his campaign. But understand this: if Alexis Daumas's house is burning, he will come to Estephan St. Pierre for help and not to you. And if Estephan St. Pierre's family is hungry, it is Alexis Daumas who will bring a piece of saltfish and some rice; not the government in the capital. You understand?' said Estephan slowly.

'But yes . . . but yes,' said Lenox, although he wished Estephan St. Pierre could have been more circumspect in the presence of his nervous candidate. 'All I wanted to know was whether we could count on you . . . whether Mr. Delaire could count on you, for a good word here and there.'

Estephan St. Pierre turned towards the candidate of the People's Alliance for Progress and smiled. 'Mr. Delaire is a good man . . . I have nothing bad to say about him.'

Victorin Delaire derived no comfort from the smile or the words of Estephan St. Pierre. A few minutes later, after detailed discussions of deaths, quarrels, weather and crops, the three men left in Lenox's car for the school grounds where the campaign would begin. Estephan St. Pierre introduced Victorin Delaire by telling the village audience about Victorin's grandparents, his parents, their origins, Victorin's childhood, his behaviour at school, his growth rate, eating habits, and other matters which the villagers wanted to know about their candidates.

When the candidate moved forward to read the speech that Lenox Marchand had written for him, the villagers gasped in admiration at the tall, thin man in white shirt and black pants, who served as a pole for the brightest tie they had ever seen. The tie bore a floral motif, blazoned in horticultural radiance that held the eye, and distracted the villagers from the vapidity of Victorin's words. At the end of his speech, they applauded with an enthusiasm that was a tribute to Delaire's courage; not, as he thought, to his winged promises. But the candidate was so elated by the response that he decided to say a few more words of his own.

'If I lose this election,' he said, 'I will go down to the bay the next day and drown myself in the sea. Tshoom!' illustrating with sound and diving motions, the effect of his impact on the Atlantic ocean. The people of Consolation desired no more. Victorin Delaire felt he would expire in a burst of spontaneous combustion.

The noise and confusion proceeded. Supporters of opposing candidates stopped speaking to each other for the duration of the campaign, and could not understand the continuing fraternization among the candidates themselves. Alexis Daumas spoke of the importance of sacrifice and working together. Victorin Delaire brought the villagers together with free beer and rum. The New Worker's Party promised better educational facilities. The People's Alliance for Progress handed out pencils to selected schoolchildren, and the parents were so impressed by the party's commitment to education, that they neglected to ask for notebooks.

The candidates and their noises washed back and forth across Palmiers and St. Pierre like intemperate floods, delaying harvests and harvesting discord. On election day, the people of Two Hills went to vote for their Alexis. The people of Consolation, believing that Victorin Delaire could not lose with Estephan St. Pierre's help, stayed home to celebrate. Alexis Daumas won the election – the only candidate of his party to do so – and would be punished by being ignored by the government for the next five years. Estephan St. Pierre was blamed for Victorin's defeat and held responsible for the anticipated neglect of the village by the government. Some villagers showed their displeasure by withholding their business from Simone's store for an entire week. Victorin Delaire did not go down to the seaside for several months, afraid that he would be expected to keep a campaign promise.

Estephan St. Pierre went to his Bible and sought comfort from the trials of Job. Maurice Jacob and Serges Jean-Baptiste came to visit more often, giving their support quietly and generously when their friend faltered, calling him back from lonely introspections. Estephan dreaded his friends' leaving, and when they did, he would hurry to bed as if that would shorten the night. Sometimes Simone would be left alone to close the store, and she would find him in bed, still awake but huddled near the wall in the shelter of the dark posts.

His reprieve came on an evening bus from the capital when Frederick Albin came home. The news went through Consolation as quickly as the bus, and when Estephan arrived, Simone did not wait for him to come into the store but shouted from the doorway, 'Frederick! Frederick Albin! He's home!'

Estephan put on a clean shirt and went to visit his old friend. There was a small crowd outside Frederick Albin's house, and he was sitting in the kitchen with his mother, Evie Albin, who held his sleeve with one hand while she moved around, as if to ensure that no one would take her son away again. Estephan pushed his way into the kitchen.

'Evie, how are you? You must be happy today,' he said to the old lady, then turned to Frederick. 'Eh, Frederick, I thought you had abandoned us. How are you, *Compère*?'

'Ay, Mr. St. Pierre, I took a little rest . . . but it was time to come home.'

'So you're feeling well now?' asked Estephan, to complete the ritual of greeting. And he sat with his friend for another hour while Frederick told them, in short, precarious sentences, his experiences during five years in the psychiatric hospital. Over the next few days, the people of Consolation looked again to Estephan to tell them when they could close their circle around Frederick Albin. On the Sunday after Frederick's return, Estephan and Simone went to his home, and the villagers saw Frederick leave with them. Later that day, word rushed through the village that Frederick Albin had eaten with Estephan and Simone St. Pierre, and had received visitors at their home. So the people of Consolation took their son back again.

Simone St. Pierre travelled to the capital on the first Saturday of every month to buy goods for her store. On those days, the villagers bought little else but bread, as

Estephan, who minded the shop then, did not know where most things were and did not know the prices of the rest. Estephan usually spent the day sitting on the small bench near the doorway, calling out greetings to anyone who walked by. He had just finished complaining about the July heat to a neighbour, when a lady he had never seen before turned from the road to the small path that led to the store. Estephan expected her to be seeking directions and withheld his greeting until she came into the store.

'Good morning, Mr. Estephan,' said the woman.

'Good morning, Madame. Are you a stranger here?' replied Estephan, puzzled by her familiarity and wondering how a woman with such a beautiful smile could have such sad eyes.

'Ah well, you may not have seen my face but we have spoken before,' she said.

'When? I'm sure I would have remembered you.'

'Oh, I'm sure you remember me, but you didn't see my face,' she said, and her smile grew brighter while her eyes seemed about to cry.

Then Estephan suddenly remembered, and his fear forced him to sit while he struggled to breathe again.

'You're the woman at the wedding party . . . that night?'

'Yes,' she answered.

'I thought I would never discover who it was. You know you have surprised me,' Estephan said. 'But what made you come here today?'

'Really and truly, I'm not sure myself. But that last time was not right . . . and it was not the right place. So I thought I would go and let Estephan St. Pierre see my face and tell him that if he ever wanted me again, I would come,' she said.

'But I don't know your name, I don't know where you live, I . . .' he said.

'You found me the last time. Eh?' she asked.

'Yes, but it was Maurice . . .'

'Well Estephan, if you want, you will see me again.'

Estephan St. Pierre poured out for her the contents of a can of grapefruit juice. After a few minutes of silence, she touched him briefly on the arm and walked out to the road to wait for a ride. When a van stopped for the woman, Estephan suddenly remembered that she had not told him her name. He ran out to the road and waved. 'Your name, you didn't tell me your name!' he shouted.

She turned and said something, but he could not hear her above the noise of the accelerating van. Estephan never mentioned those events to Maurice or to anyone else. He did not see the woman again, but was grateful that she had found a fragment of his pride and had returned it. Much later in life he convinced himself that he had imagined the woman's visit.

Chapter 6

Elfrida St. Pierre, who had lived with Madame Ferdinand since Estephan's marriage, rushed the news of Bertrand Louis's arrival in Consolation to Simone.

'But he's so sad, Simone,' Elfrida said, 'we couldn't even look at him last night. I thought he was going to cry in his food.'

Later, when Madame Ferdinand had decided that Estephan was home and that her audience was large enough, she and Elfrida took Bertrand Louis to be introduced. Madame Ferdinand wore a black dress and an expression that were both intended to dispel any suspicion of frivolity in her relationship with the apprehensive man who followed behind her and Elfrida.

The two men looked into each other's eyes and knew they had climbed the same hills. 'Mr. Louis should put himself at ease,' Estephan said, and Bertrand Louis went to sit on the bench near the door of the shop. The villagers who came to buy and to talk stayed longer than they had to, sounding out the stranger, waiting for his approval of their jokes and his support for their opinions. Bertrand Louis responded carefully, smiling when they laughed, giving reasonable support to both sides of a dispute, and winning approval from all.

In time, Bertrand Louis stopped holding his breath when the sourness of the villagers' sweat stung his nose, and he forgot the grime on their hands and under their nails. He even began to envy their comfort in clothes so stained and torn that the fabrics may have returned to the vegetation from which their threads had come. The men from the village waited for the man from the capital to offer them his past.

'I tell you,' said one, 'I believe Bertrand Louis is escaping some great crime in his family.'

'I don't know,' said another, 'but I wonder whether he has visited Madame Ferdinand's bed yet.'

'Madame Ferdinand! It would take a man of great courage to begin to think of such a thing . . . and with old Elfrida there? No,' they said.

'Eh, and he speaks English so well.'

But Bertrand Louis did not know that it was necessary to share his past and he did not say enough. So the villagers pulled him into their lives and they began to lay him bare, minutely and relentlessly.

People who lived in the village paid for goods but not for the labour of their friends and relatives. So when Estephan wanted help to butcher a goat, he sent a child to summon Bertrand Louis. When he arrived, Estephan looked at his clean clothes in wonderment. 'Ay, friend, you know what I called you for?' he asked.

'The child said you wanted help to kill a goat,' Bertrand replied.

'Yes, but you'll get dirty, you know.'

'It's OK, I'll watch out.'

'All right, hold the legs,' said Estephan.

So Bertrand Louis knelt in the red dirt to clutch the legs of the terrified animal that had become as strong as a horse. It tore his blue shirt, kicked him in the knee, rubbed it's droppings on his arms and fixed its gaze, full of pleading and reproach, on his face. Bertrand's previous contact with animals had been through his mother's and wife's cooking, and he had occasionally petted a friendly dog. When Bertrand managed to restrain the animal, Estephan positioned its head over a basin and slit its throat. Bertrand tried to look nonchalantly away, but when he felt the eyes of the 'hawk' on him, he forced himself to look at the dark red jet that was frothing in the basin and tried to let his eyes drift out of focus. The animal weakened, and he could rest his hands lightly on its legs, and wait for his cramped fingers to recover. Estephan tied a cord firmly below the hole in the animal's neck, then cut a small slit above the ankle of the left hind leg. He inserted a slender stick into the hole and moved it around to loosen the tissue below the skin, then he put his mouth to the hole and began to blow. The goat's body swelled like a hideous balloon until its legs were outstretched in supplication to the sky. Estephan drew the knife down the taught skin of the chest and belly, and along the inside of each leg, then pulled the skin back, cutting the white webs of tissue that delayed him. He spread the skin on the ground and emptied the entrails onto it; then he quartered the animal.

'Here,' he said to Bertrand, 'you take a leg and a piece of liver for you all.'

Bertrand took the meat with many thanks and little appetite, and hoped that the world would not always smell of goat.

'When Maurice passes by later, I bet he'll ask for the balls . . . to roast with salt and pepper,' Estephan said helpfully.

'I see,' said Bertrand.

One week later, Serges Jean-Baptiste called to ask whether Bertrand had any experience in making farina from cassava roots. Bertrand did not, and instantly learned that Serges and Ti-Louise would not be able to prepare the farina without him. The first day, he peeled the heavy roots, then rinsed them with water that Ti-Louise had carried from a spring two miles away. In the evening, they packed wicker bags with the white pulp and placed them under a press of boards and rocks to force out the juice that contained poisonous prussic acid. The next morning, Bertrand helped them roast the moist pulp in a vast iron cauldron. When Serges took little Nadiege to the toilet, Bertrand sat on a rock near the roasting shed, admiring the strength and stamina of the beautiful country woman. He hoped she was not going to ask him to help, when she stopped to stoke the fire.

'Bertrand . . . you're married?' she asked.

His shock made the hot day frigid. 'My wife's dead,' he said after a while.

'You have children?'

'Yes. Two. A boy and a girl. In town.'

'But we haven't seen them,' she said.

Bertrand did not know how to deal with this woman – young enough to be his daughter – who was relentlessly unearthing his past.

'Ti-Louise,' he said, 'things were very hard for me and my family. The children went their way. I came to Consolation for some peace.'

'Ah-ah, I'm sorry to hear that. I'm sorry to hear that your wife is dead,' Ti-Louise said, and turned back to the cauldron. She had heard enough for the day.

The next night when Madame Ferdinand brought his supper, she said, 'I'm sorry to hear your wife is dead. How did she die?'

'The 'flu,' said Bertrand Louis, wishing a similar fate on his landlady.

Bertrand yielded reluctantly to these forays into his past, and the next incursion came on the night they thought the world had ended. The darkness had just come, and the air was seasoned with smoke from dinner fires, when the sky turned pink, then orange, and a flaming moon arced over the village and sped towards the edge of the ocean. The animals panicked immediately and, after a few seconds of shocked silence, people added their screams to the tumult of howls and squeals. Mothers grabbed their children and ran indoors; the men ran to each other's homes, asking the same questions. Then everybody began to pray, kneeling in the road or wherever they had stopped. Father Alphonse was besieged by people wanting to make confessions, and he was rushing about asking what had happened – he did not welcome the end of the world without flights of angels blowing on golden trumpets. Estephan St. Pierre and Bertrand Louis had been talking in the store when the fireball illuminated their faces with its orange light. Bertrand gazed at the comet in awe, then turned to Estephan, who was praying in the most profound tones, 'Out of the depths, I cry unto Thee, Oh Lord. Lord, hear my voice; let Thine ears be attentive to the . . .'

'Estephan! Estephan!' Bertrand was calling, boiling with the joy of revelation and comprehension.

'Eh?'

'It's a satellite.' said Bertrand, 'It's one of these satellites the Russians and Americans have been sending up . . . I'm sure,' and he proceeded to give a brief lecture on the matter.

When he had finished, Estephan said, 'I hope you're right . . . let's go and ask Frederick what he thinks.'

Simone was not at all convinced that they had not seen a sign of divine displeasure, and would not let Estephan leave. She was kneeling behind the counter, crying and confessing to sins she could not have committed in a single lifetime. An hour later, a small delegation headed by Frederick Albin arrived at the store.

'Did you see the satellite?' Frederick asked, with a pride that suggested he had arranged the phenomenon.

'Yes,' said Bertrand happily.

'Um-hm,' said Estephan calmly, as if he saw falling satellites every night.

Later, Estephan said to Bertrand, 'Friend, you were a teacher before. Eh?'

'Why?'

'Well, when you were explaining the fireball, you made me feel like a child in class. I even thought you were going to repeat the lesson.'

'Yes. I used to have a little school. When my wife died, things stopped working. I started to drink, the children were taken away. I gave up.'

'Ah,' said Estephan, with sympathy and satisfaction.

Later during the 'Year of the Satellite', Estephan St. Pierre encouraged Bertrand Louis and Frederick Albin to write letters to the newspaper, asking why the government had not fulfilled a five-year-old promise to provide Consolation with electricity. The letters were written in such beautiful English and with logic so impeccable, that Alexis Daumas read them aloud several times at legislative sessions. Eventually, the Ministry of Communications and Works sent a truck with ten thirty-foot poles, which they dumped at the side of the road, in the middle of the village. Nothing happened for the next seven months. So a delegation from Consolation, that included the priest and schoolmaster, went to the Ministry of Agriculture to complain that the poles interfered with the transportation of crops to the capital. Next, they went to the Ministry of Communications and Works and presented the Minister with a box of fruits and vegetables and told him these would be the last produce to come to the capital: they would use the electricity poles to block the highway to all traffic to the city.

The government truck came back, and several men with grave voices and thoughtful frowns supervised the erection of the poles. The villagers readily provided the labour and food. Three months later, darkness disappeared forever from the nights of Consolation.

Father Alphonse was delighted: henceforth, there would be no nocturnal sanctuary for those committing sins of the flesh – at least not around the church. Maurice Jacob was devastated. His trysts would have to be arranged with much more delicacy as the women would have to be persuaded to walk farther from the village, and he would probably have to spend most of the time allaying their fears about snakes. Maurice had caught the smell of progress and it stank.

When the electricians had tied Madame Ferdinand's house to the brown pole that stood outside, Bertrand Louis could listen to his radio for the first time in years. He invited several friends to share the occasion, and Madame Ferdinand's home was filled with villagers about to witness yet another wonder in a cascade of technological miracles. At the right moment, Bertrand turned a knob – the radio hissed and its glass front suddenly became a bright, yellow band, arrayed with black lines and numerals. Bertrand adjusted another larger knob, and a small wand moved across the numerals, and music, squeals, voices speaking in incomprehensible languages, poured out of the radio. The villagers looked at each other in contentment, and all nodded their heads sagely as if this was exactly what they had expected. At last Bertrand stopped turning the large knob, adjusted the volume of sound with the smaller, then leaned back and smiled to show that he had an unimaginable surprise for them all. They heard a few musical notes that were not part of a song, then a man's voice said slowly and carefully, 'This is the Voice of America, broadcasting in special English.'

The party ended two hours later when Madame Ferdinand began clearing her throat, and the guests left, proclaiming their intentions of making immediate purchases of radios, and with Estephan thundering in argument with two 'stupid sons-of-bitches' who were convinced there was a tiny gramophone in the black box.

Many people in Consolation suspected that it was Father Alphonse's long hours of exposure to electric lights that sent him to the hospital. Some even thought of going back to their kerosene lamps, but when they remembered the smell and the soot and weak illumination, they decided to risk the exposure just a little longer.

Visitors to the hospital brought flowers, fruits and bags of the sweets they called 'paradise plums'. The villagers came back with reports that the hospital had made the old priest even sicker; so subsequent visitors advised him not to permit surgery under any circumstances. They entertained him with stories of surgeons leaving their instruments in the body cavities of their patients, and of their many relatives and acquaintances who had been killed by the wrong medicines given by tired nurses. They advised him to be especially vigilant for signs of fatigue in the doctors and nurses.

A young priest came as a temporary replacement for Father Alphonse. He immediately earned the villagers' disapproval when he said 'my child' to parishioners old enough to be his grandparents. At his third mass, he shook their faith when he announced that he would celebrate the next Sunday's mass in English. Even Maurice was scandalized when he heard of it from Serges and Ti-Louise Jean-Baptiste.

'God will punish that priest,' he promised, wondering whether God could understand a mass not said in His familiar Latin.

Estephan and Simone went to visit the new priest and to ask him to reconsider his decision.

'You must understand that we country people like a little time to consider new things. If we start saying mass in English, then go back to Latin when Father Alphonse returns, people will say that the Church does not know what it wants. You understand?' said Estephan.

'That's true,' said Simone in support.

'Let me tell you, Mr. St. Pierre, I understand well what you're saying, but I cannot stop the change. Already in the city the mass has been said in English for a year,' Father Nantes said.

'The city people speak English; if they want their mass in English, let them have their mass in English. But we like our old mass. There will be trouble if you change it . . . people will stop coming to Church.'

The priest nodded, pursed his lips, looked at the ceiling, and stroked his moustache. 'How about if we try it for one mass and see what the people think?' he asked.

'We can do that,' said Simone quickly, not wanting to argue with a man of God.

'All right,' said Estephan, 'but I think we'll want our old mass back.'

The next Sunday, Father Nantes said most of the mass in Latin, except the Consecration and the Lord's Prayer. The children liked it, and many adults discovered for the first time what the priests had been concealing in Latin all those years. Several people asked the priest to continue saying the mass in English. Estephan surrendered in silent disgust.

The church authorities offered to send Father Alphonse back to France when he told them he was dying. He was excited at first about returning, before he remembered the cold Christmases and the colder people.

'I don't want to die at sea,' he told the bishop, 'and arrive in France with the frozen meats. Or be thrown into an undiscoverable part of the Atlantic by some atheist of a ship's captain.'

'The bishop promised to have Father Alphonse buried in Consolation.

The old priest asked the doctor to write the name of his illness on a piece of paper – just as he had written it on the chart. He looked at the words for a moment, then with the smallest of smiles said, 'Yes, I shall feel better dying of . . . please help me with the words – pulmonary interstitial fibrosis, yes? – than dying of pneumonia. There is more dignity in the name that no one can understand.'

'It could have been the smoking, you know,' said the doctor.

'I know, I know,' said Father Alphonse, 'but that's the only vice we can enjoy . . . at least it sends us to heaven more quickly. Yes?'

The bishop's chauffeur drove him back to Consolation. It took the priest three days to find the courage to tell Estephan and Simone St. Pierre and the schoolmaster that he had six months to live – if he took care of himself. The villagers at once forgot his irascibility and all the pleasures he had denied them. Father Nantes stayed to assist the old priest and eventually persuaded him to try saying the mass in English. But Father Alphonse's accent transformed the mass into such an unintelligible liturgy, that he resolved to continue the old tradition until he died.

Madame Ferdinand had by this time, with the agency of sympathetic smiles and encouraging words, discovered that Bertrand Louis had a daughter named Lise and a son named Nicholas in the capital. So on their Saturday visits to the capital, the villagers asked shopkeepers, policemen and fellow shoppers whether they knew the whereabouts of Lise and Nicholas, who were the children of the teacher, Bertrand Louis. Many people had known Bertrand, but he had disappeared into the countryside with his children. Eventually a market vendor said she knew Lise.

'Eh-heh. It's the girl with the sweet smell,' she said.

'Sweet smell?' they asked, not understanding.

'Yes, yes. She smells so fresh. She works in Guy Chalon's pharmacy,' the vendor said.

This intelligence was discussed in Simone's store for several days. There was no news of the boy.

Nicholas Louis had been taken to England by a kind man who was still a bachelor at fifty-four. They travelled on a white and blue Italian passenger ship, and shared an oven of a cabin that jumped enthusiastically with every wave. The kind bachelor found a job for Nicholas with the London Transport Authority, and the sad, bewildered boy began methodically to forget his past and his modest ambitions in the obscurity of a flat in the greyness of north London's Tottenham.

So the villagers decided to send Serges and Ti-Louise Jean-Baptiste as their emissaries to Guy Chalon's pharmacy to try to persuade Lise Louis to visit her father. Serges and Ti-Louise saw immediately the shadows of Bertrand Louis in Lise's face. Ti-Louise, who was never afflicted with shyness, spoke first. 'You're Bertrand's daughter?'

'Yes,' an astonished Lise replied to the pretty girl with the country accent. 'What's happened?'

'We're his friends from Consolation. My name is Ti-Louise. This is my husband, Serges. Our name is Jean-Baptiste.'

'I haven't heard from my father for years, and I don't know if he wants to see me again. We had disagreements after my mother died.'

'That's OK,' said Serges, 'we want you to come for Christmas. You don't have to worry about a place to stay. You must come.'

'I don't know yet if I can go. I'm helping my godfather with the pharmacy. He has diabetes and it's hard for him to stand . . . his wife has her own work. I have to see,' Lise said. She liked the innocent forwardness of Ti-Louise and was amused by her husband, who appeared to be sniffing an elusive perfume in the air. 'But how is my father?' she asked.

'Your father is so happy,' Ti-Louise said. 'He has many, many friends; everybody likes him. When we have letters to write, he always does them for us.'

'Yes, um-hm,' said Serges.

'Everybody respects him,' Ti-Louise continued.

'Everybody,' Serges said in agreement.

'And Christmas! Let me tell you about Christmas. My God, it's so nice, so much to eat and drink, and everybody has such a good time.'

'. . . so happy,' Serges confirmed.

'Dances, music, it's so nice.'

'. . . so nice,' Serges echoed.

At this point, Ti-Louise was moved to tears. 'If you could only come to Consolation for Christmas. Your father would be so happy. His only regret is that he cannot have his children with him for the season.'

'Um-hm. For the season,' Serges said, with pleading earnestness.

Bertrand Louis was not informed of any of those machinations on his behalf. One week before Christmas, Simone visited the pharmacy to continue the negotiations.

'Ay, but of course . . . but of course.' Guy Chalon said,

greatly amused by Simone's invitation to Lise. 'The child needs a holiday. And it's not good for her to stay so long without seeing her father. I'm sorry Nicholas is in England. I'm sure Bertrand would like to see him again.'

Consolation started its Christmas celebration in the small presbytery with Father Alphonse. The villagers wanted him to see them while their new clothes were still clean. They accepted small glasses of Dubonnet and shyly refused refills, saying that they had not come to drink, but to wish him a merry Christmas. 'And you look so well, you'll probably baptize our grandchildren,' they assured him. Then they hurried to Madame Ferdinand's end of the village. Bertrand Louis and Lise were still crying together, and Elfrida was bawling in sympathy. Madame Ferdinand was revelling in all this tearful happiness. The drinking and eating began in earnest and they moved from house to house, their numbers increasing with each visit. The villagers stopped cars and buses travelling through Consolation and invited willing strangers to heaped plates of fragrant food. When the crowd arrived at Estephan St. Pierre's house, a four-piece orchestra was fiddling quadrilles and mazurkas and Maurice Jacob had begun shouting a 'verifiable' story about a man from Palmiers who was a witness in a court case.

'"At approximately what time were you there, Sir?" the judge asked in English. And before the interpreter could translate, the man from Palmiers responded indignantly, "Approximately? Which Approximately? There was no 'Approximately' there Judge. And if Mr. Approximately tells you that he was there, well, he's lying. I was the one who saw the whole thing."' Maurice ended his story with a raucous laugh.

The people of Palmiers told the same story about a man from Consolation.

By nightfall, every household had been visited and a muted Maurice Jacob, whose voice had fled from the abuse of rum and shouting, and whose previously white shirt had become a dripping, brown sash about his waist, was whispering in hoarse desperation for the fireworks. Estephan insisted that Frederick Albin set the fireworks off, as he appeared to be the only one still able to focus his eyes. For the next hour, blazing rockets tore through the night, humbling the electric lights, and endangering every house. Eruptions of a hundred colours blazed from gaily decorated volcanoes, drawing screams of approval from the children. It was a better Christmas than Lise could have imagined. She was relieved to see her father again, and she was fascinated by the tall man with the hawk-like face, and by his striking wife.

Two days later, Lise left for the capital. The villagers provided her with food sufficient for a camp of refugees, and promised that the entire village would visit her on New Year's Day. They did.

The town square was festooned with rainbows of pennants. Thousands of people came from all over the country to show off their best clothes and to eat foods that they ordinarily disdained. They milled in cheerful confusion, buying mercilessly expensive codfish fritters, fried chicken and warm beer from impatient vendors who ringed the square with booths. The children crowded into buses that drove around the city at imprudent speeds, while their passengers screamed insults at prominent citizens and indulgent policemen. Young men from the city prowled about the town square, strutting their fashionable clothes and sophisticated accents before pretty country girls. The young women, flattered by the attention, accepted rides and gifts, then ran giggling to their friends when they heard what they were expected to give in return.

Bands of masqueraders ran through the city, following a man dressed as a red and black devil, and chanting, 'Give the devil a child to eat!' while his band of smaller devils sang in refrain, 'One, two, three little children!' Crowds of children in ecstasies of terror, surged back and forth around the 'Devil', then screaming in terrified relief when they escaped his goad.

The fete continued for two days, then pungent bus-loads of drunk, tired and dirty revellers returned to their towns and villages. The people of Consolation spent most of the following week finishing leftover food and drink. Then, as soon as the hangovers and the enteric disorders subsided, they returned inevitably to neglected farms that had become slightly unfamiliar.

Father Alphonse died in March. His housekeeper said that she heard him laughing loudly during the night, then he had stopped after a fit of coughing. In the morning, he did not answer when she knocked, and she entered to find him dead. And smiling. Time had kept Father Alphonse in Consolation for so long, that he had become a piece of the valley, like the river and the road. But the church would not allow a wake, and the villagers felt that their mourning was left wanting, and their sorrow was stained with resentment. Father Nantes weathered their hostility at his presumption in replacing their old priest; he waited patiently until they were ready for him.

One evening, Estephan St. Pierre and Bertrand Louis went to visit the young priest, to ensure that he knew his place in the village and would not set about changing everything. Estephan was going to be pushed only as far as the English mass. The priest was in the school playground shouting instructions to a horde of small boys pursuing a football with violent purpose.

'Gentlemen!' he called, and came hurrying over. 'Is anything wrong?' Their sombre faces made him anxious.

'Oh, nothing's wrong,' said Estephan, 'just came by to see how things were at the presbytery.'

'Fine, fine. I'm trying to get a good football team here, so we can massacre Palmiers's team.'

'Palmiers has a football team?,' they asked.

'Uh-huh.'

'Then we mustn't use your time. If you need any help, just let us know.'

The left, talking excitedly about a football team that would beat Palmiers's bunch of unwashed criminals and bring fame to Consolation. When the friends gathered in Simone's shop to discuss the day's news, only Serges Jean-Baptiste showed any interest. Maurice Jacob and Frederick Albin were distracted by titanic emotions: they had breathed the perfume of forest water, and impossibly beautiful visions of Lise Louis filled their minds.

Chapter 7

No one in the village could have explained precisely how the men knew when it was time to fish with the seine in the bay. Some insisted they could smell the fish; others claimed that they could see schools of fish as black stains in the water. Nor could they explain to the priest why the best fishing days happened to fall on Sundays. Father Nantes mentioned his concern once, and the men shook their heads in amazement at the miraculous coincidence. They admitted there were some things they had no power to change.

Nine men accompanied Estephan St. Pierre to Great Hole – their wives and children would come later to help with the cooking and carrying the fish. The seine, which they had left to hang on poles just inland from the beach, under the sea-grape trees, was carried by four men to one end of the beach. They anchored one end of the seine by two ropes to a stake in the sand, and the rest they loaded into a dug-out canoe that they rowed in a great arc around the bay to the other end of the beach. Four men at each end of the seine began hauling the long crescent, grabbing schools of fish from the bay. Estephan and Maurice were rowing back and forth along the edge of the seine, beating the water to keep the fish within the trap, when someone called from the beach that the net was stuck. They rowed back over a shallow reef, and Estephan slipped into the water and swam slowly over the coral shelf, which was only two feet below the surface. He freed the net from the branches of a mass of staghorn coral and swam back warily over colonies of black sea-urchins whose six-inch-long spines waved in warning at the shadow that passed over them. He thought he heard someone calling his name, and he lifted his head out of the water to see Maurice rowing frantically to keep the canoe from foundering on the reef. On the shore, people were screaming at him to swim into the deeper water, into a wave that rose like a hissing darkness towards him. He realized immediately that if the wave broke over him while he was in the shallows over the reef, he would be shredded on the coral spines and edges like a piece of cassava on a new grater. As the wave closed in, it drew water from the reef and Estephan felt the sea-urchin spines enter his chest and belly and thighs like hundreds of lighted cigarettes being extinguished on his skin. He was too frightened to think of the pain and dived down into the base of the wave, trying to get beneath its pull. For seconds he remained motionless at the edge of the shelf; then, as he was about to surrender in a scream of panic, the wave released him and fell in angry frustration on the reef. He shot to the surface and gasped as if to inhale all of the air above the bay, but he had opened his mouth too soon and his lungs were burned by the saltwater that rushed in. He almost drowned then, retching and trying to breathe, when Maurice grabbed his arm and pulled his head above the water. For several minutes he coughed and gasped, and was so weakened that Maurice had to pull him aboard the canoe, risking overturning the unsteady boat.

The villagers had been so badly shaken by the near disaster that they had abandoned the seine. Those people who saw death so often, in its guises of illness and events called 'the hand of God', could not reconcile themselves to its inevitability; there were too few of them and they were too close. Some of the men were crying when Maurice ran the canoe aground and helped Estephan ashore. Estephan coughed up some more water and laid still on the hot sand until he had regained sufficient strength to notice the agony from the spines embedded in his flesh. He rolled over and they saw the small punctures on his skin, bleeding from their black centres. Someone tried to remove some of the spines, but the barbed needles entered more deeply whenever they were touched.

'So we came here to bathe the seine?' Estephan asked when he could breathe normally again.

'Estephan, we thought we had lost you.'

'Me, I am not ready,' he said, trying to smile.

'I don't know where the wave came from, look at the sea – not another wave.'

'That's true, the wave came from nowhere, no warning, nothing.'

'. . . no warning. Nothing.'

'Ay-ay-ay, I've never seen such a thing.'

Estephan wanted them to get back to the seine and salvage something from the day, but the joy of hearing their endlessly repeated words was too important at that moment, so he stared at the sea and let their voices give him strength again. There was sufficient fish to provide a meal for each participating family, but not enough left over to sell.

Simone stayed up all night with him, rubbing hot tallow over the points of indescribable pain on his body. Next day, the pain prevented him from leaving his bed; then fever came, and that was joined in two days by a coughing that clawed at his lungs. Simone's herb teas, and warm honey with lime and rum, did not help, and after four days Estephan allowed Simone to call a doctor.

'We're only going to pay a lot of money for nothing. I am already getting better.'

'Look at me, Estephan. I am not letting you die in this bed. You're burning up with fever and that cough is killing both of us,' Simone insisted, and she sent a message with the driver of a morning bus to the health clinic that served the East coast.

The young, handsome doctor who came the next day did not wear a tie, wishing to show his oneness with his people. It was only his stethoscope, draped in casual declaration around his neck, his black bag and expensive black Rover that proclaimed his status. Simone found it difficult not to look at him when his face was turned away, and was so disturbed by her thoughts that she was relieved when he made preparations to leave.

'Your husband has pneumonia, Madame St. Pierre. You will have to go to the city for his medicines. Here's the prescription. I'll stop by tomorrow. You can pay me in a couple of days.' The doctor spoke quickly and seemed to have trouble getting his breath.

Simone let him see himself out. 'You see?' she said to Estephan, 'You almost died.'

'Just a bad cold,' Estephan replied.

Dr. Clement Michel had to drive fifteen miles to his home. When he was five miles from Consolation, he had convinced himself that he felt no impure attraction for Madame St. Pierre. Ten miles from Consolation, he was certain that his attraction for Simone St. Pierre was no more than that of a connoisseur for a fine painting. By the time he reached his home, to be met by the familiar pleasantness of his wife's face, Simone's beauty had become a torment. He spent an impatient night constructing strategies to meet Simone St. Pierre that were as detailed and tortuous as the most complex surgical operations. The next morning, his eyes revealed that he had wrestled with demons and lost.

Three days later Dr. Clement Michel stopped to see Estephan St. Pierre. 'You'll be fine in another week, Mr. St. Pierre,' he said, 'but please take it easy. Your body has had a hard time.'

'Ah, you're right, I think the old body needed a rest,' Estephan replied, determined to get out of the bed as soon as he was sure the doctor's visits had stopped.

On his way out, Clement Michel stopped to talk with Simone St. Pierre in her shop. He suffered intensely waiting for an admiring customer to leave, and spoke quickly before someone else came.

'Mr. St. Pierre is doing well enough now . . . but he is a very healthy man. I'll come and see him in a week, but

I am sure I'll have to go and search for him in the bush,' he said.

'That's true. But thanks a lot. You've taken good care of my husband,' Simone said.

'Madame St. Pierre . . . please do not take this the wrong way. I say this with all due respect: you are the most beautiful woman I have ever seen.' Clement Michel stopped, in great apprehension and with some surprise that he had had the courage to say those things to Simone St. Pierre.

Simone looked at him in astonishment, then laughed softly. 'My husband said the same thing to me twenty years ago. You men are all the same. Now go and say that to your wife.'

Clement Michel left feeling like a child who had been gently rebuked in class by his teacher. Simone St. Pierre was so disturbed that she wanted to go and bathe immediately to wash away the thoughts that were shouting in her head. For the first time since she had met her husband, another man had made her wet herself.

Simone was angry when she saw the doctor's car stop outside her store one week later. But she had to admit to herself that she would have been disappointed if he had not come. Clement Michel had rehearsed his statement for Simone St. Pierre so many times, and had driven himself into such a state of agitation, that when he entered the store he forgot everything that he had planned to say. Every reasonable phrase, every polished word, turned to air and disappeared at the doorway. The two people stared at each other in confusion until Clement Michel remembered that he was a doctor.

'How's the patient?' he asked, pressing his arms to his side to stop the cold streams of sweat that were dropping from his armpits.

'He refused to stay in bed. Said he had too many things to do, but two boys went with him to take care of the animals,' Simone replied.

'Madame St. Pierre, when do you go to the city?' Clement asked picking up a thread of courage.

'The first Saturday of the month. Why?' she replied.

'The next time you come, please have lunch with me.'

'At your home?'

'No, no, the Hotel Ste. Anne. It's a nice place . . . very nice,' he said.

'Dr. Michel, I don't know if that is a good thing. And I am so busy when I come to town. I don't know.'

Clement Michel left a bottle of antibiotic tablets and took away an exaggerated fragment of hope: she had not said 'no' to his invitation and she had not chased him out of her store. During the following days, he examined her last statement, 'I don't know', in the minutest detail. He repeated to himself every imagined nuance in her tone. He recalled her expression. He even considered the position of her hands when she spoke. His obsession with Simone made him impatient with his wife, to the point where he occasionally entertained fantasies of a distraught policeman bringing him the sad news of her sudden death in a traffic accident. The thought of having to raise two daughters made that fantasy less pleasant, and the callousness of the illusion disgusted him. It made him feel undeserving of Simone St. Pierre; so he began considering reasons for his wife to desert him. But he found it impossible to fashion a circumstance where she would leave quietly with the two girls, determined to make no future claims upon him. Even more difficult, was finding a way of enticing Simone from her husband; maybe he could persuade her with the temptation of a comfortable life in the city. This assumed a measure of co-operation from Estephan St. Pierre that would be difficult to obtain: St. Pierre would most likely kill him.

Simone St. Pierre amused herself with fantasies of lunching with a handsome lover at the Hotel Ste. Anne. She had no intention of accepting Dr. Michel's invitation. The people of Consolation would forgive a man's infidelity and tolerate or even admire a suspicion of his infidelity, but they would never forgive a woman's. She shivered when she considered the scandal that would follow the discovery of Estephan St. Pierre's wife with another married man; it would be worse than finding the priest in bed with a twelve-year-old girl. She was flattered by the doctor's attention and wondered whether Estephan said similar things to other women. So she unleashed the demons of suspicion that waited on the edge of her thoughts, about Estephan's withdrawal from her. It was not natural for a man to be so long without a woman; he had to have some release. Yet Simone, who had the village's most receptive ears for gossip, had heard nothing untoward about her husband except concerning his quick temper. And even if he could live with deprivation, it was not fair that she should live the rest of her life without the enjoyment of a man. For several weeks she participated in breathtaking fantasies in which she and Clement Michel met in the most romantic rendezvous, where they undressed each other with the utmost delicacy, then proceeded to enjoy themselves in screaming, violent heavings that lasted many hours.

Then she surrendered. On one of her Saturday trips to the city, she completed her shopping two hours early, then took a bus to the town where Dr. Michel had his clinic.

'You're not from around here, Madame?' the nurse-receptionist asked.

'No,' Simone replied, 'but Dr. Michel asked me to see him here at half past one. Please tell him I am here.'

Clement Michel asked the nurse, in the calmest tones, to send Madame St. Pierre in. When he saw Simone St. Pierre standing in his office, Clèment almost cried in gratitude. Her plain, navy-blue dress was more captivating than anything his wife had shown him in her Sears Roebuck catalogue, and her faint perfume brought gardens of roses into his little office. These provided sufficient encouragement for Clement Michel to pour out – in a hoarse whisper, so that the nurse would not hear – wave upon wave of compliments that compared Simone favourably with the most popular screen actresses and several goddesses of Greek mythology.

'Dr. Michel,' Simone said, wanting to dam that river of names she had never heard, 'I have to go in a while to catch the bus home.'

'It's OK, I'll drive you home,' he offered.

'Another time,' Simone said, and that small promise caused such a surge of hope in Clement Michel that Simone saw the arteries pulse in his neck and his forehead shine with new sweat. Before she left, she let him hold her hand briefly and kiss her on the cheek.

Simone visited the clinic three months later, and that time agreed to let Clement Michel drive her home. Clement had time to convince himself that Simone St. Pierre could be seduced and he had carefully planned a detour along the way. He suggested that they stop at a small beach that was famous for its protective mangrove and sea-grape trees. She did not object to that, nor to his kisses, nor to his triumphant removal of her clothes. He slipped out of his own and stared in the purest admiration at the beautiful woman lying along the back seat of his car. He positioned himself carefully over her as if this were a sacred ritual; but, as her entered her, she pushed him off and rolled away.

'I cannot do that,' she said, and began crying so strongly that he did not have time to feel frustration or anger.

'Take me home please,' she asked.

'Please, please, please,' he kept saying, not understanding what had happened. 'Simone, please stop crying. I know this is the first time. The next time we'll manage better.'

Simone turned to him and said in a voice that he did not like, 'You want me to do that again? I'll not even be able to look at myself in a mirror. For the rest of my life I'll have to lie to my husband and myself.'

'You love your husband a lot, Simone?' Clement asked.

'You city people are always talking about love,' said Simone. 'You love your arm or your leg, Clement Michel? We country people don't marry for love. Estephan married me because I came from a good family and my father had told him that he had a beautiful daughter. Estephan didn't marry me because he loved me. He married me because I was suitable . . . and for me, he was suitable.'

Clement Michel listened to Simone with such sadness and helplessness that he was almost relieved he had not taken her. Later, he would regret not having been more persuasive and patient. 'I'm sorry,' he said, embarrassed by his inadequacy.

'I'm sorry enough for both of us,' Simone replied.

They drove to Consolation, and Simone buried her face in her hands so that she would not be recognized by someone on the few buses and cars they met. She prayed that Estephan would not see them arrive, so that she could go in and wash her face, but he was standing in the doorway of the store.

'You had better come in,' Simone said to Clement Michel.

'You've arrived,' said Estephan in greeting.

'I'm tired,' she said, waiting for Estephan to see her guilt and recognize it, and was surprised when he looked past her and smiled at Clement Michel. 'Will the doctor stop for a little something?' he asked.

'Just for a minute,' Clement Michel replied. 'I saw Madame St. Pierre waiting at the bus depot and asked her to travel with me . . . I'm going to see a patient in Two Hills.'

'Who is it?' asked Estephan.

'Don't remember the name. Somebody's going to meet me at the roadside, near the school,' Clement Michel replied. He did not feel he could continue lying much longer, and hoped that the grimace on his face was accepted as a smile.

Simone walked quickly to the house, too afraid to look

back, believing that Estephan would be staring at her in disbelief and screaming, 'Whore! Bitch!' She heard him laughing and shouting goodbye as the doctor's car drove away. She washed her face very carefully and changed into another dress.

'How was town today? asked Estephan when she came back into the store.

'Same difference . . . it was so hot today,' she replied.

'Nice fellow, that Clement Michel,' he said.

'Uh-huh, but he drives too recklessly,' Simone St. Pierre said.

That night, Simone dared not touch Estephan in bed, afraid that her sin would soil him. The night extended itself pitilessly, telling her over and over that she was the most contemptible woman in Consolation; and it showed her the scarred faces of prostitutes in the city calling her name with obscene familiarity. She had anticipated nightmares, and they came with a virulence that made her want to rush out of the house and not desecrate the home that Estephan St. Pierre had built. She must have awakened Estephan during her pitiful sleep because she remembered his asking during the night, 'You can't sleep?' By morning, she had decided to go to confession, but she could not go to Father Nantes. She could not reveal such a sin to their priest. So she searched for an excuse to return to the city. She kept remembering items she should have bought; then complained that she had been over-charged for flour and rice, and wondered whether she had ordered sufficient cloth and thread. On Thursday, Estephan shouted in exasperation, 'Why the hell don't you go to town and give me some peace? You malediction!'

On Saturday, Simone went to the city and fled to confession in the Cathedral, where she told a priest over and over again, 'I've never done this before to my husband.'

The tired man, who had received this assurance so many times that he didn't have to wonder about an adequate penance, said automatically, 'Say the rosary five times today.'

Simone was slightly disappointed that her confessor had not been shaken by the vileness of her sin. She considered going to another priest but was afraid that the first priest would see her, so she decided to double her penance to compensate for his shortcoming. Then she began her atonement with the purchase of two work-shirts and one dress-shirt for Estephan, and resolutely denied herself anything.

In time, Simone stopped feeling faint whenever a black car stopped near her store; she even began feeling a slight sympathy for Clement Michel. When her searching ears detected no hint of scandal, and her status in Consolation remained unchallenged, she would occasionally release the remembrance of her affair, enjoying the wickedness of playing out the fantasy to a conclusion that quickened her breathing. She was even pleasant to Clement when he stopped at the shop three months after their meeting to give her a box of Danish assorted biscuits.

'You don't have to do that,' Simone said, hoping that he had killed any wish to see her again.

'It's only a small gift for a good patient,' he replied.

He had turned to go, when she asked, 'You're well yourself?'

'Fine, fine,' he replied.

'And the family?'

'No complaints.'

'That's good, you must stop and see us again,' she said, and regretted it immediately.

'You mean that?' he asked.

She shrugged and said goodbye with great courtesy.

When Estephan came home, she handed him the tin of biscuits.

'Your doctor brought these for you,' she said.

Estephan picked out the biscuits with red jelly centres. 'I hope it's you he likes and not me,' he said, directing a cannonade of laughter at Simone, who found it difficult to smile under fire.

Clement Michel bathed his hurt pride with comforting words. You win some, you lose some, he reminded himself, trying to enjoy recollections of past conquests, with their trumpet blasts of passionate inanities that had driven him to gasping, sweating frenzy. He was incredulous that he had let his greatest prize slip away with only the weakest protests. It would have been so easy if he had only held her down, or if he had threatened her with exposure. So his lust sat in judgement and decreed that he could redeem his self-respect only with the payment of Simone St. Pierre's virtue.

The young doctor found very good reasons to stop at Simone St. Pierre's store when Estephan was away. Usually he would buy a can of fruit juice, which he always pronounced refreshing, despite the lack of ice. Then he started bringing gifts from the city, which Simone refused with thanks and itching regret. When his great expenditure of time and money did no more than amuse and enrich Simone, he turned to mild threats. 'Simone, you know well you're killing me. All I want is to spend an hour or even a half hour with you.'

'Maybe you should see a doctor,' suggested Simone.

'You're not worried that your husband finds out you've been with me?'

'And how, Mister Doctor, is he going to find out?' asked Simone in anger.

'You know,' he answered.

'Then he'll kill me . . . and you too,' she assured him.

'I'm sorry, Simone, but I cannot leave you alone until we finish what we started.'

'You better not come into my shop again!' Simone almost screamed in anger and fright.

Her fear and guilt were so great that she almost wanted Estephan to find out, so that he could beat her and throw her out. Then she could fling her disgrace and abandonment in Clement Michel's face and still refuse him. In desperation, she sent a neighbour's child to ask Ti-Louise Jean-Baptiste to visit her.

Of course . . . I hear he's always in your shop,' Ti-Louise said mischievously. 'You two have a little thing going?'

'Ti-Louise, enough joking. The man is trying to make me go to bed with him. He's even talking about letting Estephan hear that we are having something.'

'Ay, God. I can't believe that. And he looks like such a nice man,' said Ti-Louise. 'Uh-uh, I'm going to discourage him.'

'What are you going to do?' asked Simone.

'That man cannot come to Consolation and take what he wants. You have done a lot for us. We'll fix him.'

Serges Jean-Baptise was horrified and enraged that the wife of the man who had saved his life was being threatened. After two days of careful thought, he suggested a plan for dealing with the situation that was so good Maurice Jacob felt a twinge of envy, but he could make no improvements.

Dr. Clement Michel received an urgent message from a bus driver that a woman at Consolation was very ill with fever, chills and sweats and was passing black urine. She was too ill to be transported. Clement Michel grabbed a syringe and a bottle of quinine for what he believed was a case of cerebral malaria, and left to meet the boy who would be waiting at the side of the road. He was driving past the last house at the south end of village when a boy waved at him to stop. The child said only, 'You have to run,' and sped off.

Clement Michel followed the sound of the child's calls of 'Come' as well as he could, for two miles into the growing darkness until they came to a small hut, from which he could hear a woman groaning softly and a man crying repeatedly, 'Don't let her die.'

Clement Michel pushed open the door and rushed into total darkness and silence. The door was thrown shut, and two arms embraced him with such power that he did not even attempt to struggle. He was pushed to the ground, face down, and he felt a machete against his neck.

'Don't even think of moving and don't open your mouth or I'll shit in it,' a man's voice said. Someone else sat on his legs and he felt the pressure of his belt ease suddenly as a knife cut through the leather; then his pants and shorts were pulled down to his knees.

'Turn him,' another man's voice said. The first pair of hands turned him over, and their owner sat on his chest and pressed the machete against his larynx.

'OK,' said the second voice, and a third person walked across the room and Clement smelled the remnants of body powder and assumed it was a woman. A pair of softer hands grabbed his genitals and he felt the blade of a knife against his pubic bone. He gasped and was about to scream when the first voice said, 'No!' and pressed the machete down. At that point Michel lost control of his bladder, and he heard a woman's voice say, 'Merde!' and his stream of urine was directed into his pants.

'He's wetting himself,' the woman whispered.

'He better not do anything else,' said the second voice.

'Clement Michel was beyond all horror. He was so certain of death that he had actually grown calmer, and he was thinking curiously of what his final second would feel like, when the first voice spoke.

'If you ever, ever, trouble Madame St. Pierre again, we will cut this out and send it to your wife with an explanation. Now put on your clothes and go. You better run . . . it's getting dark and we don't want you to hurt yourself. Drive carefully and go and take care of your wife and children.'

The concerned voice did not calm Clement Michel and he did not follow the advice to be careful: he bruised himself against every bush and rock along the almost invisible path. He was trembling so violently that he could not change his car from first gear for ten minutes. He did have the presence of mind to stop at the clinic before he went home, and remained for an hour in the toilet vomiting. When he arrived home, he had already entered a long period of abstinence.

Simone occasionally saw Clement Michel's car drive by. He never stopped for a drink in the store, and Estephan wondered with some disappointment why he had stopped visiting. 'You'd think we did something to him,' he said.

Ti-Louise and Simone never spoke of the doctor again. Maurice Jacob hesitated to offer that joke to Heaven.

The surfeit of tranquility to Simone St. Pierre's life permitted her to return to prying into the affairs of her neighbours. Her first assignment was to deprive Maurice Jacob and Frederick Albin of the pleasures of bachelorhood. She had seen both men turn to motherless puppies in the presence of Lise Louis, and she thought that the more sophisticated Frederick Albin would be a better match for the city girl. There were two complications that delayed and irritated her: Frederick had been to the madhouse, and Maurice Jacob possessed energy and appetites that would soon exhaust any normal woman. She decided to deal first with Maurice, in a plan whose deviousness was fostered by the success she had had in saving her body and soul from Clement Michel. She waited one night until Estephan had fidgeted himself into a comfortable position in bed, and asked, 'Estephan, don't you think we should ask Lise to come and stay with us for Easter?'

'Um-hm,' Estephan agreed. He went pleasantly to sleep, thinking of the way Lise made the house smell of hill forest in the early morning – she should have been his daughter.

Lise Louis enjoyed the celebrity status she found in Consolation as a city lady and guest of the St. Pierre family, but she would not consider leaving the city and its diversions, and she found it easier to love her father at a distance. She arrived on the evening bus on the Thursday before Easter, and the people who considered her theirs were standing in the shop doorway and sitting on the steps. After the embracing, came the question which they all had to ask: 'You're well?'

'Yes.'

'And your godfather?'

'He's the one who's well.'

'And his wife, she's well?'

'Very well.'

'You don't like Consolation? We hardly see you.'

'Don't say that; I am so busy in the pharmacy.'

'. . . busy in the pharmacy,' they agreed.

The questions would be asked again and again while they searched her face and voice for hidden worries and hesitations, eager to share the sorrows and failures of the girl who smelled of forest water.

On Good Friday morning, the cocks, grackles and bananaquits ignored the solemnity of the day with calls as joyful and raucous as on all the mornings before. The day was hot and dry, like all the Good Fridays anyone in Consolation could remember. After mass, they ate the traditional lunch of mackerel, rice, cabbage and carrots. In the afternoon, the children – who had been made to forgo games and other entertainment – were allowed some respite with pieces of dry, brittle *pain d'épice*, the spice biscuit strongly flavoured with ginger.

On Easter Sunday, Estephan and Simone St. Pierre, Lise Louis and their friends carried the pots of food they had cooked the night before to the bay, for a day-long picnic. Maurice Jacob set about impressing Lise by carrying twice as much as anyone else and would have carried her if she had shown any signs of fatigue. At the beach he offered her unceasing supplies of fruits and fresh coconut-water. When they went into the water, Maurice became an encyclopedia of survival techniques and swimming styles; he even put his shoulders at her disposal if she needed a springboard to dive into the shallow water. Frederick Albin hovered at the periphery of the whirlwind around Lise for two hours before he could say a word to her; but, because of the company nearby, he could only ask politely how she would like living in the country.

'It's too late for me to change now. I don't think I can leave the city, but I don't want to stop coming to spend time in Consolation,' she said.

'I used to work in the city a long time ago . . . I went to school there,' Frederick Albin said.

'You think you could go back?'

'For a good reason . . . yes,' he said, in a voice shivering with hope.

Then Maurice Jacob's voice and enthusiasm swept Frederick away. Simone St. Pierre had seen everything and had decided that she knew what was best for everyone. So she asked Estephan to remind Maurice that perhaps Lise would like to talk to her father and to Madame Ferdinand. On the way home, when everyone was trying not to look ahead at the road that led uphill from the beach, and which had grown steeper than they remembered, Estephan asked Maurice to walk with him.

'Eh, what do you think of Bertrand's daughter?' asked Estephan.

'But the woman can make a man crazy. Every time I stand close to her, I want to throw her down on the ground,' Maurice replied fervently.

'I think she would make a good wife,' suggested Estephan.

'Um-hm. But you know, a man should try her out first. How do I know . . . you know what I mean?'

'And after you've tried her, you'd marry her?'

'You remember my mother and father?' asked Maurice, 'Did you ever know two happier people? And that's because my father refused to get married. Ehhh, I am not going to make any woman miserable with marriage.'

'Maurice,' Estephan said in the voice that seemed to come from the ground, 'don't spoil life for Lise; let her find a man who wants to marry her.'

'You know, *Compère*,' Maurice replied, 'you've just

spoiled a good plan I had for getting Lise to go pick rabbit food with me. But you're right, she probably wouldn't want to talk to another man after me.'

'Uh-huh,' Estephan replied, with a little smile that acknowledged a joke heard before.

The following Saturday, Frederick Albin spent the day in the city and came back with only a newspaper and a paper bag. Then he began travelling on weekdays as well. Once, he stayed in the capital for three days. Even the village children discussed that. No one was surprised when Frederick Albin announced that he had found a job in the city and would take his mother to live with him.

Chapter 8

The Seventies brought changes to Consolation – like stones flung without cause or remorse. The trucks came first – small Japanese trucks as brightly coloured as ripe mangoes. Estephan St. Pierre considered the purchase of every vehicle a personal affront and a blow to his status in the village. He warned so often about the stupidity of mortgaging family lands to pay for the 'dangerous maledictions', that the villagers joked that he should be consulted before peeing. Then came the transistor radios whose sharp noise pursued people to forests where even silence had been loud before. On Sunday mornings, the village road became a confusion of speeding vehicles, carrying screaming radios and young women and driven by recent veterans of adolescent wars with pimples and fickle voices. Suddenly, other beaches far from the scrutiny of parents, were bluer, calmer and safer than those at St. Pierre, and on holidays, Consolation was left to the old, the poor and the prudent.

Then 'Molasses' bought a car. Molasses, whose name was Clement Pascal, had come by his nickname since the day, fifteen years ago, when he had tried to steal molasses from a pig farm. He had unwisely selected a drum lying on its side and had hastily removed its bung, unaware that the contents of the drum were under pressure from the gases of fermentation. The thick, odorous syrup had flung itself at him in affectionate vengeance, and had turned the astonished boy into a fragrant semblance of Lot's wife. Fear of discovery had prevented him from washing the molasses off at the farm, and he was forced to sneak back into the village. He tried to run to his home but was hampered by clouds of bees, flies, and most of the village children, who were loudly proclaiming his new identity.

Molasses, who Estephan thought could never justify his existence, had stolen eggs from some of the villagers' hens, had tortured their dogs, had impregnated a twelve-year-old blind and crippled girl, and had – Estephan said – sucked his mother's life out with her milk. Molasses had somehow persuaded his adoptive father, Aristide 'Brazil' Pascal, to buy him a car.

Aristide was eighty-nine years old and the second oldest person in Consolation. The oldest villager was Courbee the leper, whose disease had eroded her face and limbs, but whose disfigurement repulsed death until she was one hundred-and-one years old. Aristide was called 'Brazil' because he had once lived in that country for three years. He left, he said, because a politician had grown jealous of his influence in a *favela* in Belem and had tried to have him assassinated.

The truth was that he had left his country to work on the construction of the Panama Canal. Three days after leaving port, the ship's ailing cook died of dysentery, and the captain, afraid that the rest of the crew was diseased, offered the cook's position to the passengers. Aristide was the only man among them who showed any interest in the job, and so he became a seaman.

When the ship arrived in Belem, Aristide deserted to stay with a prostitute whose obscene vocal embellishments to her writhings in bed convinced him that he was an incomparable lover. In gratitude, he spent the next three years trying to convert the woman to a state of Christian purity that he himself could not achieve. Eventually, the recalcitrance of the woman and the ridicule of her customers drove him to enlist again as a cook on a small, decaying freighter that took him to Colon in Panama. There, he worked for five years shovelling apart the continents of North and South America. He returned to his country with enough money to buy one hundred acres of land, which overlooked the ocean but which were incapable of sustaining anything but acacia shrubs and cassava.

Brazil was sixty years old when he persuaded a young, childless widow from Palmiers to live with him. Two years later, Molasses was born, and Brazil protested to all that he was not the father. The mother refused to say who the father was, and it was only after her death nine years later, that Brazil formally adopted the boy.

With cunning and determination, Molasses became a retribution for every sin his father had committed or even contemplated. He stole constantly from the old man, abused him when he protested, but was strangely protective and would readily fight anyone who made the slightest criticism of his father. It was as though he reserved to himself the sole right to hurt the only one who had given him anything.

Molasses required only one week to persuade Brazil to sell ten acres of land to buy a Mazda sedan that was more expensive than any house in Consolation. Estephan St. Pierre soon learned of the source of money for Molasses's new car and went to visit Brazil.

'I hear you're tired of breathing good, clean, fresh air,' Estephan called in greeting.

'Eh. It's you,' said Brazil. 'Listen, when you get to my age, your body starts to hurt out of spite.'

'. . . out of spite,' Estephan agreed in sympathy.

After fifteen minutes of enquiries into matters of health and weather, Estephan asked, '*Compère,* you think it was a good thing to sell your land to buy Molasses a car? And the most expensive car in the country?'

Brazil looked down at the ground for a long time before he answered. 'Estephan, I don't have too much time left, and when I go, the child of the devil will get everything. Let him sell the land, let him buy cars. I'll get some peace before I die.'

'I understand, but . . . never mind. I just cannot stand to see our land going to banks in the city. Anyway, God is love.'

'Yes. God is love,' Brazil said.

A new car can quickly become as essential to life as food and water, and Molasses drove his car from conquest to willing conquest. When he became a father for the second time, his explanation to the father of the fifteen-year-old girl was that she had insisted on showing him her 'motions'. The totally unsympathetic father and his two sons beat Molasses unmercifully, but were so awed by the dazzling car that they did not touch it. Molasses was so relieved that he did not even consider revenge.

After a few weeks, when his bruises had faded and the villagers had stopped laughing, Molasses resumed his activities, but was more circumspect in his dealings with women from St. Pierre. It then became customary to assume that Molasses was responsible for all untoward occurrences in the valley whenever another culprit could not be found. And so, when the body of a little girl was found a mile from the village, obviously assaulted sexually, and with her face battered beyond recognition, the villagers immediately suspected Molasses. Someone must have notified the police, because the next day, two policemen were seen talking to Molasses and examining his car minutely, collecting dust from its floor and seats, and dusting the passenger area for fingerprints. By the time the police left, most of the village had gathered around Brazil's home, and some men in the crowd were muttering that Molasses should not be allowed to sleep in Consolation another night. An old woman who lived nearby was wailing loudly that her virtue was now in peril – although the unpleasantness of her face and nature had made her virginity impregnable for fifty-five years. Molasses was not seen outside his home for the next two days.

Four days after the incident, Estephan St. Pierre was awakened by a soft and insistent knocking at his door. 'Mr. Estephan . . . Mr. Estephan,' a voice called, in a terrified whisper.

'Who's the person?' Estephan shouted.

'It's me, Molasses.'

'Molasses?' Estephan asked in astonishment.

'Yes. I'm sorry to disturb you and Madame Simone, but I have to talk to you.'

'Don't go,' Simone whispered, 'the man's a murderer.'

'No. I'd better talk to him,' Estephan said, and went out. He considered arming himself, but his machete was in the shop, and if Molasses wanted to murder him for no reason, he would not be so polite about it.

'Molasses, what do you want at this hour?' Estephan began.

'Mr. Estephan, I didn't kill the little girl,' Molasses said quickly.

'Why are you telling me that?'

'People in the valley want to hang me. You're the only one I can expect to give me a chance.'

'Me? Molasses, I am not a lawyer . . .' Estephan protested.

'Please help me. Please tell me what to do. I didn't do it. I swear on my mother's grave.'

Estephan wished fervently that that most contemptible of persons had found someone else to favour with his entreaties, but knew instinctively that Molasses was telling the truth.

'Tomorrow, I'll go with you to town to find a lawyer.'

'Thank you, Mr. Estephan. Thank you,' Molasses said, and his voice did not have its usual mocking tone.

The next day, Estephan rode in silence and discomfort with Molasses to the capital, in the beautiful red Mazda sedan. The two men went to the law office of Gregoire Chastanet, Bachelor of Arts, Doctor of Law, Queen's Counsel, whose father was distantly related to Estephan. The eminent and busy attorney did not see them for an hour, but when he came out into the waiting-room, he welcomed Estephan with a warmth that suggested frequent practice.

'I don't believe it! Mr. Estephan St. Pierre in my office at last! How is Simone, that beautiful lady?'

Estephan grinned helplessly. 'Not as well as you,' he replied.

'Ah, don't do that to me,' Gregoire Chastanet said in a show of profound regret. 'Now what can I do for you?'

Estephan introduced Molasses, and began to explain,

when Gregoire Chastanet interrupted and said with a sad smile, 'I know, yes . . . yes. The story is all over the country . . . a bad crime, a bad, bad crime. But have you been charged with anything, Mr. Pascal?'

'No, but the police said I was the only suspect they had.'

'Well then, I cannot do anything until you are charged with a crime, you know. Then as a favour to my good friend and my cousin, I can consider taking your case. But Mr. Pascal, these things can be very, very expensive. I'm warning you.'

Two days later, Molasses was arrested and charged with the murder of the little girl. The police said they had a witness, and that they had found threads in the defendant's car that matched the fabric of the victim's dress.

Now that the people of Consolation faced the reality that the worst of crimes had been committed in their valley by one of their own, their anger at Molasses was extended to all outsiders. They resented the rest of the country for thinking that a person of Consolation could have done such a thing. It was unfair: they were good, kind people. And they began to say that Molasses was probably innocent.

Neither Aristide Pascal nor Molasses could afford the lawyer's fees, so Aristide gave Gregoire Chastanet the title to his land, on the understanding that they could continue to live on it until Brazil's death. Estephan served as a witness and intermediary for the negotiations. This satisfied everyone except Estephan, who insisted unsuccessfully that the Mazda should be sold to pay the lawyer. The car remained locked in a shed near Brazil's house, and Molasses went to the prison in the capital.

The crowd that gathered outside the court-house for Molasses's trial decided it would be an intolerable miscarriage of justice if Molasses were not hanged. They heaped abuse and threats on Gregoire Chastanet, whom they considered an accessory to the murder of a child who had been an angel on Earth. Several in the crowd claimed to know Molasses personally and hinted that it was not his first murder. One woman proclaimed that the cold-blooded killer had fathered twelve children in three years and had already raped his four oldest daughters.

The trial was delayed because the witness could not be found. The next day, the buttress of the prosecutor's case against Molasses was found cowering in an abandoned outhouse, clutching a little girl's underclothes. On the way to the capital, the man, a vagrant who walked from village to village doing any unpleasant work in return for food and rags, confessed to killing the child. When the news reached the reassembled crowd around the court-house, cheers rose in acclamation of Molasses's innocence – which no one could remember having doubted. Many in the crowd wondered how the police could pick on a good, decent man whose only crime had been to buy a nice car. They shouted for Molasses to be compensated for the torture the police had undoubtedly inflicted on him. The crowd waited for Molasses to walk out of the court-house with his lawyer, who was smiling modestly; and many tear-stained faces assured the celebrity that they had never doubted his innocence and that God would bless him for his fortitude and patient suffering.

Some weeks later, Gregoire Chastanet came to Simone's shop. He sat on the bench near the door and exchanged pleasantries with Simone until Estephan arrived from his farm.

'Ay! It's you,' said Estephan.

'How is it? How is it?' the lawyer greeted him with professional eagerness. 'I want to talk to you about an arrangement I had with Brazil Pascal. He's offering me three acres of land to pay my fees for the case.'

'Have you seen the land?'

'Well, it's got a good view of the bay . . .' Gregoire began to say.

'And that's all. You won't even grow weeds on it . . . but

if you want a good view, it's the best place in St. Pierre,' Estephan said.

The lawyer looked down the valley and focused on the white dots that marked the waves on the ocean. Then he said softly, as if to himself, 'Yes, a nice view for old eyes and hard minds.'

After a few seconds of silence, he looked at his watch and said in surprise, 'Look at the time. Madame Simone, thank you for putting up with me for all this afternoon. Cousin, I think I'd like a little house overlooking the bay. Well, goodbye everybody.'

'Take care of yourself. Carry yourself well. God bless,' they called after him.

Gregoire Chastanet stopped near Brazil's home but did not call out or knock. He stood at the roadside, staring at the most beautiful landscape he had ever seen, feeling – like other men from the city who stopped to look at Consolation – despair with his life and an obsessive want for the women who smelt of limes and the sea. Three village children came by to stare at him, followed his gaze and, seeing nothing but the curve of the bay and the edge of the ocean, began a studious examination of the interior of his car. He turned around at the sound of footsteps and smiled at the young woman who was walking towards them.

'You're looking for something?' she asked.

'No, no. Just looking. Just admiring the view,' he said.

'The view? Oh. Yes, it's the best place in the village to see the beach. Sometimes you can hear people's voices all the way from the beach.'

Gregoire thought of the noise of the city, the impatient harshness of car horns, and the stink of gasoline, diesel and stale perfume. He thought of the pious assurances of the criminals who provided him with a comfortable living, and his dazzling wife who had abandoned contemplation and effort for gossip, parties and servants. Even with his limited time, he found time to read, while his much-admired wife embarrassed his home with romance novels and libellous tabloids. A man like himself needed more – a comfortable weekend retreat, an understanding country girl, like the one talking to him, to keep him company.

'What's your name?' he asked.

'Sylvie James,' she answered.

'I'm Mr. Gregoire Chastanet,' he said proudly, 'the lawyer who got Molasses out of trouble.'

'Oh. I've heard of you,' she said, a little surprised that such a personage would talk so easily to her.

Gregoire Chastanet straightened himself to his full height of five feet, ten inches and said, 'I may be putting up a house here. I hope you don't mind me for a neighbour.'

'True? No, no. That would be nice,' Sylvie James said, anxious to get back and spread the news.

Gregoire drove back feeling like the hero at the conclusion of one of his wife's novels. By the time he arrived in the city, he could already envision his weekend retreat. He saw his Saturday nights spent cavorting with Sylvie James, who could not do enough for him, in gratitude for the money, jewellery, clothes and perfumes he would pour on her. And when he got tired of her, there would be all the other village girls. Life was going to quite satisfactory indeed. He was grateful that he had no children.

Brazil Pascal gave three acres of land to pay for his son's legal defence, and sold the lawyer an additional two acres. He spent the following three months quietly watching as a redwood building with an abundance of glass, angles and posts, grew on a slope that was secluded from the road and his house. He wished the carpenters would work more slowly so he could spend more time watching them. He was grateful for the distractions that kept his mind away from death and Molasses. His memories of Brazil and Panama had been reused so often that he was no longer certain that he had been to those places. When the building was finished, he would insist that Molasses drive him to the city for a last visit. He could no longer remember the street names or even what the cathedral looked like.

Gregoire invited Brazil, Estephan and other prominent villagers to the blessing of the redwood-and-glass wonder. All the villagers attended. Father Nantes performed the ceremony but felt uncomfortable with the perfumed crowd of city people. So he left as soon as he could fashion a suitable excuse. He, too, was an exile from the city, and knew well why a man like Gregoire Chastanet would decide to build such a house in Consolation. The priest wondered whether he should beg God's forgiveness for having blessed the house of sin, but would forget his concern when his cook told him she had cooked pumpkin soup for supper.

Josephine Chastanet smiled tolerantly at the groups of eager country folk and resolved to stay away from Consolation unless Gregoire fenced the house off and restricted entry to the servants only. This was not the sort of place where her friends would want to spend their weekends, especially when they had to walk a quarter of a mile to the beach.

There was enough rum to make the village people think well of Gregoire Chastanet. Maurice Jacob saw the house as the venue for many enjoyable celebrations, but decided to allow the lawyer to settle in before discussing the matter. Estephan St. Pierre was gratified that he had been instrumental in bringing Gregoire Chastanet to Consolation, and he shared his proprietary advantage with anyone who paused near him.

The following Saturday morning, a large van with house furnishings followed Gregoire's car to the new house in Consolation. In the evening, he strolled over to Sylvie James's home.

'Sylvie! Strangers!' a voice said when he was still twenty feet from the house.

Sylvie walked around from the back of the house.

'Who was that?' Gregoire asked.

'My mother. She's blind. But she can hear what you're thinking. How are you? You're well?'

'Yes. Very well. And you?'

'OK,' she said.

'Listen, you think you can come and help me arrange things?'

'Of course,' Sylvie said eagerly, impatient to enter the house that had come from an American colour magazine.

They worked late into the night and accomplished little, but succeeded in bumping into each other so often that Gregoire convinced himself that Sylvie was signalling her readiness for him. He congratulated himself on the flawless execution of a masterful plan, but decided to savour his triumph by allowing things to progress slowly. He drove Sylvie home at one o'clock the next morning.

Within two months, Sylvie James was cooking dinner for the staid lawyer, teasing out in-grown hairs on his face, plucking his grey hairs and rubbing his back when he imagined that the muscles were sore. She progressed to doing things to him in bed that made him scream in ecstasy and wonder, and which left him so exhausted that only his pride stopped him from begging for respite. He knew that her skills had to have come from long practice, but he hesitated to pry into her life for fear that he would not like what she would reveal.

One Saturday, he arrived at Sylvie's home carrying an expensive case of cosmetics. He wanted to share his celebration of successful negotiations on behalf of an American textile firm, Ultimate Cottons, that would be building a factory in the capital. He walked quietly towards the house and was surprised as usual when Sylvie's mother called out, 'Sylvie's not here, Stranger!'

'When is she coming back?' he asked.

'I don't know,' she replied with a tone that said the conversation was finished.

'Tell her Gregoire wants to see her,' he called back and left. There was no response.

His disappointment became a deaf jealousy when, by midnight, she had not called. He went to bed and imagined several logical reasons for her long absence. It was too late and too dark for her to come to his house anyway. He awoke at five o'clock in the morning from a sleep that had provided no rest, and as soon as he thought it was permissible to visit a neighbour, he drove to Sylvie's home.

'Sylvie's sleeping,' the hated voice called out as he approached the house, 'come back later.'

At noon, when he had fully resolved to tell her that he no longer wanted to see her, he saw Sylvie coming up the walk to the house. He looked at her drawn, tired, but still pretty face, and he forgave her instantly. Her disordered hair and her thin rayon dress, through which he could see that she wore only low panties, made him want to leave his wife and profession for the country girl.

'Where were you yesterday?' he asked as soon as she entered.

'I went to see a friend in Two Hills.'

'What time did you get back?'

'Late, I had to wait for a ride.' She went into the kitchen. 'You want your breakfast or lunch now?'

'I ate already,' he said. 'Look, I could have come for you if you had left a message.'

'How can I leave a message for you? Call your office or your wife? I cannot wait every weekend for you to come. I have other things to do,' she said with an impatience she had never shown him before. When he touched her and tried to make her laugh with a silly, dirty joke, she pushed him away. 'I don't feel like it,' she said. Then she went into the kitchen, where he could hear her washing the dishes he had left on the table.

Gregoire Chastanet decided it would be safest to leave matters where they were and to wait for the anger to die away. So he went out and walked to the road. Finding the effort pleasurable, he continued slowly until he could see

Simone St. Pierre's shop. It was too late to turn back now, and Estephan was sure to be offended if he did not come in to exchange greetings.

Maurice Jacob, who was sitting on the steps of the shop, saw Gregoire first. 'Eh-eh, I didn't know lawyers could walk,' he said.

'Who, Gregoire?' Estephan asked.

'Um-hm. He's coming up the road. Sylvie must have given him a break.'

'You know,' said Estephan, 'this man should be smart enough to know better than to get mixed up with a girl like Sylvie.' Then turning to Simone, he said, 'But what is it you women of Consolation do that drives these city men mad?'

When Simone had overcome her shock and confusion, she spoke indignantly. 'Why don't you mind your business? You're always trying to tell people what they should do with their lives. One of these days, your interference is going to bring trouble into this house.'

'Oh, shut up,' Estephan replied and looked around for support, but Maurice was cleaning his nails with a broken matchstick, and Serges was lost in contemplation of the horizon.

Gregoire was content to sit with Estephan on the small bench near the door, letting their conversation displace his depression until he felt strong enough to take his mind off Sylvie. After an hour he excused himself, despite protests from everyone, and started back to his house.

Maurice rose, stretched and said, 'I'll walk a little bit with you.'

When they were out of earshot of the others, Maurice asked, '*Compère*, what's wrong with you? You look like the father of misery.'

'Nothing much . . . just a little problem with Sylvie.'

'Well, you will have to fix that yourself.'

'Maurice,' said Gregoire, 'you know Sylvie well?'

'Um-hm.'

'What do you think about her . . . about her and me, I mean.'

'Well, my friend, that's one of the things a man should find out for himself, but let me tell you this: when you are enjoying Sylvie, keep a piece of yourself for yourself. That is all I have to say.'

'What are you telling me?'

'Sylvie has obligations.'

'What obligations? Is that all you're going to tell me?'

'Um-hm,' said Maurice and stopped. 'Good. Now walk carefully and carry yourself well.'

'I'll see you. Thanks,' said Gregoire.

When he got back, Sylvie had cleaned the house and left. He considered driving to her home and inviting her for a drive, but the thought of her mother's voice calling, 'Sylvie. Strangers!' discouraged him. He drove home slowly, cursing himself for wasting his emotions on a simple country girl. After all, she had only been a diversion, an easy one at that; as people said, the women of Consolation were easy. It should not be any trouble to get another one. Paul Benoit had two daughters who were beautiful enough to scratch a man's heart. He smiled as he let thoughts of his wealth, fame and good looks wash over him, cleansing his mind of Sylvie James.

His forced good humour fled when he entered his house. His wife welcomed him with a pointed stare at his feet, as if to warn him not to track dirt into the living-room. He almost wished she would discover his affair, and was surprised that a well-meaning friend had not yet given her a detailed account of his weekend activities. He suspected she did not really care. What could he do with the country girl? Marry her?

Sleep stayed out of reach for hours. He saw Sylvie's face everywhere, especially the small, round dimple just below the right corner of her mouth, that flickered just as she was about to smile. He heard her 'haw-haw-haw' of a laugh that was always embarrassingly loud, and amused him more than the cause of her laughter. Before he fell asleep, Gregoire Chastanet knew that, despite their different circumstances, he had become obsessed with Sylvie James. She had given herself freely to him and had asked for nothing in return, she had accepted his gifts with quiet delight, but had never shown disappointment when he brought her nothing. So different from his own life, where he was paid for listening to a client. He did not visit Consolation for two weeks, determined to rid himself of his obsession. But he was relieved when his wife warned that he had better go back to ensure that the villagers had not stolen all the timbers from the house.

When he arrived in Consolation, he drove past Sylvie's home to signal his arrival, then he went to his house to wait for her.

They sat in wooden rocking-chairs in the balcony and said little for about an hour. Gregoire was content. He was happy to be with the woman who gave him peace, with the clean and quiet of the country, and with the expectation of feeling her hands and mouth searching his body later in the evening.

'You're staying tonight?' he asked.

'No,' she replied, after a long pause.

'How come?' he asked in a voice that had to be forced from a throat constricted with fear and surprise.

'There's nothing in this for me. You're married.'

'But you knew that. Why should it change anything for us?'

'Look at you. A big-shot lawyer. Do you think you would let your friends see you with a girl from Consolation? Mr. Chastanet, tell the truth – you want only one thing from me.'

'What do you want me to do Sylvie? Divorce my wife? Marry you? And don't call me "Mr. Chastanet". I'm not going to see you again?' He was now thoroughly alarmed.

'You know where I live,' she said.

'That's not what I mean. You won't sleep with me again then?'

The dimple came and went quickly, but she did not smile.

'I'll come and . . . I don't know. Maybe.'

'Sylvie, look at me. Something has happened and you've changed. Tell me what it is and I'll leave you alone. Now what is it?'

Sylvie James stared at him for so long that he was forced to look away. Then she spoke so softly that he had to strain to hear. But he heard every syllable. 'I'm pregnant.'

For a few seconds, he felt as if he had fallen from a great height. Then he said in shock, 'But I always used something with you.'

She nodded, and he realized what that meant. 'You mean you're pregnant by another man?'

She nodded again. For a moment, Gregoire Chastanet struggled between anger and relief. Then his pride swept away everything and he shouted, 'You whore! Who got you pregnant?'

This time Sylvie smiled, then said calmly, 'I'm not a whore. Maybe for you, I was, but I'm not a whore. Don't call me that again.'

Gregoire retreated before the calm dignity of the simple country girl and said calmly, 'I'm sorry. I want to take that back. I'm very sorry. Please tell me who.'

'Molasses,' she said.

'Molasses!' he screamed in total disbelief, then rage. 'I think you'd better go now.' He was barely able to control his anger. He wanted to beat her until she aborted the baby, then find some fitting punishment for Molasses. 'How could you let that useless bastard touch you? A man who has never done anything worthwhile in his life.'

'Maybe not for you. But he's the one who made sure my mother and I always had enough to eat. I owe him. You're just like my father. He left us when he saw my mother going blind. Well . . . carry yourself well,' she said and walked towards the road.

Gregoire wanted to stop her and keep her in the house until they were both calm again. Jealousy was making Sylvie so desirable that he was beginning to tremble. Then he saw once again the arrogant, grinning, gap-toothed face of Molasses; the face that was almost wrenched away by the hangman's rope. He let her walk on until she disappeared around some trees. She did not look back.

He was so angry that he left without locking the doors of the house, driving away in a flurry of dust and gravel. The powerful car roared through the village, and was seen off with shouted curses from surprised villagers who were forced to leap out of its way. He did not even slow down when he arrived at the coast, where the road was a grey scratch along the sides of the yellow cliffs, and he was almost off the dangerous portion of the road, when a man carrying a bundle of poles turned to look towards the sound of the speeding car. A bamboo pole swung towards the car, and Gregoire pulled the steering wheel hard to the right to avoid the pole. The rear wheels skidded on the fine sand that the wind had scratched from the cliffs, and the car sheared through a barrier of *Gliricidia* trees. It left the ground and turned over and over as it rushed to the rocks three hundred feet below. Gregoire Chastanet became calm before he was thrown against the roof of the car and lost consciousness. His last thoughts were of Sylvie walking away, and he regretted that he had not said goodbye.

At Gregoire's funeral, two women mourners stared at the grey-haired man with the face of a hawk, wearing an ancient black suit and standing back from the crowd at the grave.

'Wonder who he is?' one asked.

'Don't know, but he's making me want,' said the other, giggling.

'See a wife?'
'No.'
'Let's go talk to him.'
'OK.'
Estephan saw the women look at him and laugh. His face burned with shame as he thought they were laughing at his old suit. He turned away as they started towards him, and he went to join Molasses and Sylvie, waiting for him in the red Mazda sedan. He decided on the way home that he was going to buy a new black suit, and he was going to grow a beard. Yes, he would grow a beard. That was in the same month that the strangers came to Consolation.

Chapter 9

Josephine Chastanet returned to Consolation for the second and last time, to supervise the removal of furnishings from her dead husband's country retreat. Some of the villagers recognized the widow and went to offer their condolences. They left when Josephine became too busy to talk to them, and as Ti-Louise Jean-Baptiste reported, 'She didn't seem like a woman in mourning at all. Can you believe she was wearing blue pants and a yellow top?'

The villagers shook their heads in sadness.

Life did not change significantly for Josephine after Gregoire's death. Their marriage had been an inevitability, and a vindication of her belief that she would marry a man who would allow her to live as comfortably as her parent's money had allowed her to. So she settled down to enjoy her enviable inheritance, to grace social gatherings, and to wait and select an appropriate companion from the men who would be calling soon. They would come to show their concern for her and to warn her against the cupidity of rival suitors.

Three weeks after Gregoire's death, she received a letter from the owner and manager of Ultimate Cottons, that expressed his deep sorrow over the death of her dear husband and a wish to view the 'country cottage' if she intended to sell it. The next day, Josephine called an attorney at Gregoire's old firm and asked him to arrange the sale of the house in Consolation. That took care of her last irritation. The American textile manufacturer and his wife arranged to borrow the key to the house, and were able to visit it without the distraction of a sales pitch. A small band of children guided them to the house, then raced back to tell the village that white strangers had come to Consolation.

Roy Parker and his wife, Ellie, stopped near the house

and stared in silent wonder at the overwhelming beauty of the valley that went down to the Atlantic.

'Oh my God!' Ellie said, 'I've never seen anything like this, not even in a picture.'

'This is fantastic . . . fantastic,' Roy Parker said reverently, 'what do you think?'

'I'm hooked,' his wife replied.

'Nicer than Galveston Bay, you think?' he asked.

'Shoot, Roy. Please!'

'Let's have a look inside.'

They were in the kitchen when they saw the young woman walking slowly towards the house.

'Visitors already,' Roy Parker said, and went into the balcony. 'Hi there,' he called. 'We're looking over the house. Live around here?'

'Yes, not far,' she said.

'My name's Roy Parker. This is my wife Ellie. We're from Texas.'

'My name's Sylvie' she said, and paused at the bottom of the steps.

'We're thinking of buying the place. Did you know Mr. Chastanet?'

Sylvie hesitated long enough for them to know that she had been more than a neighbour. 'Yes, he was my friend. I used to help him cook . . . and around the house.'

'Well maybe you can take care of the house for us when we're away,' Ellie suggested.

'I don't know,' said Sylvie, 'I'll have to ask my boyfriend.'

She had already decided to come back to the house and to try and atone for her guilt over Gregoire's death. If they had not quarrelled, he would probably be on his way to see her now. Anyway, she liked the man with his long sorrowful face, and his small plump wife, as round as a child's ball and dressed as colourfully.

'It has a nice view,' Sylvie said. 'Sometimes you can hear voices all the way from the beach.'

'Really?' they said.

'Um-hm,' Sylvie assured them. Then she missed the old friend with whom she had shared that observation in another time.

'Great. Well, see you,' said Ellie Parker, and the Texans resumed their examination of the redwood house.

Sylvie rushed back with the news that people from Texas were coming to live in Consolation. Maurice Jacob was sceptical. 'You say he's not very tall, and he's wearing shorts, and his wife is small and fat? No, I don't know where they come from, but it's not Texas.'

'So Maurice,' said Serges Jean-Baptiste, 'all Texans are seven feet tall?'

'Well, all the ones I've seen,' Maurice replied.

'And all in the cinema,' Simone St. Pierre said.

'No . . . not only there,' Maurice said, but he did not explain further where he had encountered multitudes of tall Texans.

On their second visit to Consolation, the Parkers visited Father Nantes. 'We're thinking of buying Gregoire Chastanet's house. To have a place for the weekends. Getaway sort of thing.'

The priest nodded, 'Nice view. I blessed the house when it was built.'

'Really?' Ellie Parker said brightly.

Father Nantes frowned slightly, as if wondering whether they doubted him.

'We came to see you,' Roy Parker explained, 'to find out a little bit about Consolation. You know, who's important here, what sort of reception you think we'll have. That sort of thing. You know.'

The priest was unable to suppress a grin. 'I've been here so long, that I feel uncomfortable in the city now. And even with people from the city. I came to replace the old parish priest. He died of lung disease and I had a bit of a hard time at first. The old people didn't know what to do with a young priest. Well, there's a fellow here, Estephan St. Pierre, who's like a mayor. Nothing official. But his family settled this valley and the place is named after his family. He's an interesting character, proud as hell ... excuse me ... he's impatient, outspoken, but he's a good and generous man. He believes it is his obligation to protect Consolation. The young people laugh at him behind his back, but no one will dare stand up to him. Except maybe his wife, Simone, a very nice lady. I warn you not to make an enemy of St. Pierre. He belongs to this place. Even his enemies would stand up for him. I'm sorry ... I didn't even give you a chance to talk.'

'That's all right,' Roy Parker said. 'That Estephan sounds like a really fascinating character, but we'll take your advice. What we want to know is, what can we do to fit in. Look, we're obviously foreigners and there are lots of things we don't share, but we like this place, and we're going to be here for a couple of years. We want to fit in without too many waves.'

'Please, Mr. Parker, the people of Consolation are like people everywhere – good ones, greedy ones, thieves, saints, and so on, and so on. But on the whole, they are the most sympathetic people I've ever known. After living here for a while, you find that you have become part of a family. You cannot leave. Look around you, maybe not too much to impress you, but I myself, I want to die here.'

'Well, we couldn't have got a better testimonial,' Roy Parker said.

'One thing before you go,' said the priest. 'Don't try and buy these people; they'll take your money and laugh at you. God bless.'

'So what do we do?' Ellie asked when they got back to the car.

'No big deal, we go see the honcho, sweet-talk him. Everybody's got a price.'

'You're not going to try and bribe the man?' Ellie asked.

'Not with a penny. Let's go see the guy.'

Estephan was not in when they found his home, and Simone suggested that they return on Sunday, after mass.

Word had already spread through the village that the strangers would return to Consolation to speak to Estephan before buying the glass-and-redwood house overlooking the bay. Popular opinion favoured the strangers moving to Consolation. Besides the entertainment they would provide, it meant that Consolation would at last be recognized for its beauty and tranquillity.

There were about seventeen villagers standing around Simone St. Pierre's shop when the Parkers arrived. Estephan was sitting in a rocking-chair on the balcony of the house, near the old rose bushes. He was trying hard to appear nonchalant as he puffed on an old pipe, but found himself refilling the bowl more often than usual.

Simone brought the Parkers to the house and returned to the shop to share her impressions of them. Then the crowd moved to the balcony. Estephan St. Pierre seated his guests, and sat back. This was as it should be.

'It smells so beautiful here,' said Ellie Parker.

'Yes,' said Estephan. 'The roses. They've been here before I was born.'

'Really!' Ellie said.

'Now. I hear you're thinking of buying Gregoire Chastanet's house. He was my cousin, you know,' Estephan said.

'Oh. Didn't know that,' said Roy Parker. 'Good man. Handled some important legal matters for us.'

'Yes,' said Estephan and, not wishing to explain his part in the circumstances that had brought Gregoire to Consolation, asked, 'When are you planning to move here?'

'Oh soon. We wanted to have an idea of . . . well, you know, how the people here would think about white Americans coming to their village.'

Estephan smiled proudly and looked at the audience. 'You hear that everybody?' he said in their French dialect. 'Haven't we always welcomed strangers?' Turning to the Parkers, he said, 'We don't have time for this foolishness of hating people because they look different. When people are too poor, they can't afford to waste anybody. No, come to Consolation. Enjoy yourselves. People here respect you . . . if you respect them.'

Roy Parker thought he heard a clear and polite warning in that statement.

Simone St. Pierre brought them slices of a heavy, almond-flavoured cake and glasses of gin and coconut-water. Ellie drank so many of these, that she assumed the appearance of a rotund, beatific angel unable to take flight from her chair.

Estephan St. Pierre thought he had managed that last crisis with aplomb. He had certainly been more successful than in his encounter, a week earlier, with two students who had returned from Canada for the Christmas vacation. They arrived wearing trousers with grotesquely flared bottoms, and sporting immense 'Afro' hairstyles. At first he had thought they were entertainers. When Simone explained who they were, he berated them from the doorway of the shop; then went to complain to their parents. It had been an unpleasant hour for all but the students, who became immediate setters of fashion for the young people of Consolation. In a few weeks, even Serges Jean-Baptiste was wearing bell-bottomed trousers, and Estephan was left muttering obscenities about those incapable of little but, 'Thinking foolishness, talking foolishness, and wearing foolishness.'

The Parkers bought the house at Consolation, and Sylvie agreed to look after the house when they were in the city.

'You think Chastanet had something going with Sylvie?' Roy asked Ellie shortly after they had moved in.

'You bet he did. And she's pregnant,' Ellie replied.

'Really? Couldn't tell,' Roy said, 'but she sure is cute.'

'Uh-huh, Ellie said, 'you can look all you want, but if I catch you messing around with any of the country girls, I'll blow your balls off.'

Roy gave her a look of profound sadness and asked, 'And what do I do if I catch you bouncing around under one of the country boys?'

'Then,' Ellie said brightly, 'you can blow *his* balls off.'

'Sure,' Roy said.

One Sunday morning after breakfast, Roy Parker stood on the balcony, staring down the slope of Brazil Pascal's land to the beach at Great Hole. He had hesitated to mention it to Ellie, but he thought that if he could persuade the old man and his son to sell them the whole barren estate, he could transform it into a small colony of luxury holiday homes for expatriates. Ellie had taken to walking barefoot around the house, and even her accent was changing slightly. He knew she would be unhappy about turning a piece of Consolation into a tourist resort. But, what the hell! Progress was progress, and he estimated clearing one and a half million dollars if he retained control of the development.

Later in the week, he telephoned a business associate in Houston and invited him to visit them.

'I swear to you, Bob, this place is absolutely fantastic. There's no way I can begin to do it justice. Breeze blows all the time, not too much rain, beach nearby. Just perfect. I tell you, we can really wrap up here. Haven't said anything to Ellie about this, though; she's gone all native and protective about the place. Even talks like them now.'

'How do you get along with the people there, though?' Bob Farelle asked.

'Oh, just great, they're OK folks. Just have to remember to say hello and ask how they're doing, and how's the family. That sort of thing.'

'Well let me think about it. I'll call you back. Give my love to the little butterball,' Bob Farelle said, laughing.

'Up yours!' Roy Parker said. Then he leaned back and sighed contentedly.

When he got back to the apartment where they lived

while in the city, Roy said, 'Spoke to Bob Farelle today. I went on a bit about the place at Consolation and he asked if he could come down for a couple, three days. Said OK.'

'He's going to have a fit, no sauna, no golf course and nobody here to admire his American Express Platinum card,' Ellie said. 'Is he bringing one of his floozies?'

'Knock it off, Ellie, Bob's OK.'

'Just teasing.'

When Bob Farelle arrived, it was eighty degrees Fahrenheit, and he was sweating slightly, so he removed his bright yellow blazer. It had been one hundred and five degrees in Houston when he left, but it had not been necessary for him to leave an air-conditioned atmosphere.

'Not too bad,' he said to Roy Parker, 'over a hundred in Houston . . . thought it would be hotter here.'

'Thought so too, before I came,' Roy said. 'Sometimes you want a sheet over you in the mornings. A ceiling fan is all you need here.'

'So let's see this Shangri-La of yours.'

Bob Farelle whistled softly when they arrived at Consolation. 'Jeez, Roy, you and Ellie have got yourselves a good thing here. Realize the fortune you two are sitting on?'

'Yeah, and we'll keep it this way. Eh Roy?' said Ellie.

Roy smiled faintly, 'Somebody else is bound to come along sooner or later, and do something with it.'

'Hey! What are you guys up to? Don't tell me Bob came down here to buy this place up. What's he going to do with it? Casinos? Brothels? Hideaways for the rich and famous?' Ellie asked. She wanted to spit and discard the fear that was a bad taste in her mouth. She saw the bay crowded with beach towels and plump bodies reeking with suntan lotion. In the mornings, she would be awakened by 'Yee-has,' instead of crowing cocks and squabbling grackles.

'Cool it, Ellie!' Roy said impatiently. 'Nobody's said

anything about spoiling the place. The whole point is to keep it just like it is. That's what makes it special.'

Ellie went into the kitchen for a few minutes, then returned smiling. 'Got an idea,' she said. 'How about asking Sylvie to cook a special local dish for us? We've never tried any of their food.'

'Yeah, good idea,' Roy said, relieved that Ellie had turned her interest to food.

'Sure . . . great,' said Bob, with an enthusiasm that was insincere.

Sylvie returned from Simone's shop with the ingredients for a soup. An hour and a half later, she told Ellie that she had made them a *callaloo.*

'What the hell kind of a name is that?' Bob Farelle asked.

'What's in it, Sylvie?' Roy asked.

'Salted pig's feet, pumpkin, okra, dumplings, callaloo leaves and spices,' she said, with the joy of displaying a treasure.

The three Americans blanched. Ellie suddenly wanted to settle for toast and coffee, but she said bravely, 'Well, let's see it.'

Sylvie placed a tureen of thick, green soup on the table, and went back into the kitchen with Ellie to get the tableware.

'If you don't like it,' she said, seeing their discomfort, 'call me and I'll come for it.' And she went home.

Roy and Ellie nodded bravely. Bob Farelle thought he would never again feel hunger. After some consideration, Ellie decided to taste a small portion of the soup, and when she did not fall down dead, Roy tried some. The first swallow made the passage of the rest of the callaloo easy; and later, when they sat in the balcony sipping gin and tonic, Ellie said, 'You pigs . . . didn't even leave a drop for Sylvie.'

'Now, let's talk, Roy,' Bob Farelle said.

So in a mood created by Sylvie James, who gave easily

and seldom thought of asking for anything in return, the greatest changes of all came to Consolation. The rest of the world had discovered the small village that overlooked the Atlantic, whose inhabitants would have been amused to learn that others would pay great sums to swim in Great Hole or to sit and stare down the valley of St. Pierre.

Bob Farelle left two days later. Ellie had finally surrendered.

At the airport, Bob said, 'Look Roy, I'd keep this thing pretty close. One word and they'll want a couple hundred thou' for the place.'

'Heck, I'm not that dumb,' said Roy Parker, and they shook hands.

It was Maurice who suggested that they invite Roy to an agouti hunt. Estephan thought it was ridiculous and that the American would decline, but Roy Parker immediately agreed. On the morning of the hunt, he was waiting at the shop when the others arrived. They gazed in admiration at his immaculate safari suit and desert boots that were being worn for the first time, and were suddenly embarrassed by the old clothes that they reserved for hunting.

'You're going in the bush like that?' Estephan asked.

'That's all right, that's what these clothes are for,' Roy replied.

For an hour and a half, Roy tried bravely to keep up with men who spent their days farming steep hillsides or working cultivations ten miles from their houses. Fatigue appeared foreign to them. His thirst had become so painful that he turned away when the men kneeled to drink from the small forest streams, but he resolutely refused any water offered to him. It was only when they paused to plan their strategy that he noticed no one carried a gun.

'How are you going to catch the agouti?' he asked.

'Oh, the dogs will run it down, and we'll grab it before they can eat it,' Estephan said.

'I see,' Roy said, looking doubtfully at the half-starved dogs that were scarcely bigger than rabbits.

The men stopped at a small clearing on the slope of a small valley. When they wandered off to refresh themselves, Roy noticed that Estephan walked into the woods away from the group and out of sight. He decided to follow Estephan, as he wanted some sense of the old man's feelings about his own plans for the valley that led from Consolation to the bay. He stopped when he thought he heard a cry of intense pain. He almost called out in alarm, but forced himself to walk quietly towards the sound. Estephan was leaning against a tree, with his forehead pressed into the bark as if trying to pass on an agony that had twisted his face into a grotesque mask. Roy Parker waited until the groaning stopped, then walked noisily towards Estephan. 'Hi! There you are. Anything interesting?' he called.

'No,' Estephan said, 'just a minute . . . I'm coming.'

When Roy had relieved himself, he sat on a fallen log as if to regain his strength. Estephan paused nearby. 'So how do you like living in the bush?' Estephan asked.

'I tell you,' said Roy, 'when I wake up on a Monday morning, and it's just rained, and everything smells fresh, I don't want to leave for the city. It's just hell to drive to the city. Ellie surprised me . . . I thought she would find it hard to live away from a city . . .'

'So she likes it?' Estephan asked.

'Loves it!' Roy said.

'Loves it,' Estephan repeated contentedly.

As they started back, Roy asked, 'You know, Estephan, Pascal's place doesn't seem good for any crops. Don't you think he should put it to some other use, like . . . uh . . . housing?'

'People at Consolation don't need more housing,' Estephan said.

'I mean like holiday apartments. For people from the city . . . people from abroad. All that's there now is Pascal's old house and a lot of that weed with the red leaves.'

'If you cut away the *ti-baume* and put houses there, the

rain will wash away the soil. At least Pascal can still use it to plant some manioc,' Estephan explained patiently.

Roy was thinking of some way of reopening the subject when they heard the men calling, 'Estephan-oh! Roy-oh!'

The hunting party did not catch any agouti. There was not even a sighting. The dogs cornered two opossums in a tree, and one of the men climbed up and knocked them down with a pole. Roy Parker declined politely but resolutely the offer of one of the animals, although the men assured him that it was a special delicacy. They even offered to prepare it for him, but the American protested that Ellie was expecting him for supper. The others tried to hide their relief; one opossum would not have gone far among them.

So Roy Parker returned home with no game, but with a multitude of cuts and bruises, heat rash, torn clothes and shoes that would never be repaired. He told Ellie that he had enjoyed himself.

Alexis Daumas was beaming as he walked towards Simone's shop. Estephan was keeping his Saturday morning vigil, while Simone persecuted her suppliers in the capital.

'Mr. Estephan, how is it, how is it?' he called.

'At last,' Estephan replied, 'Ti-Alexis, we don't see you again, we don't hear from you. How's the wife and the children?'

'All well. All well,' Alexis Daumas said. 'I've heard some interesting things about Consolation. Soon you're going to be a big city.'

'What are you talking about?' Estephan asked.

'Eh-eh. I thought you were part of it. The American who lives down by the sea just signed an agreement with the government. He bought Pascal's land and is going to turn the place into a holiday resort.'

For a long time Estephan stared at the politician, saw that there was no joke, then he closed his eyes. He waited for the noise of confusion in his mind to die down; and when he spoke, his voice came with a tremor that he could not hide. 'And so our guests are making us servants,' he whispered.

Alexis Daumas sat next to Estephan on the small bench near the door. They did not speak for fifteen minutes, then Estephan asked, 'Too late to stop it?'

Alexis nodded and looked at Estephan; he saw a sadness that was beyond the comfort of tears or anger. There was nothing more to say, so he said his goodbye softly and touched his friend's arm. The old man tore his gaze from the beach at Great Hole and said, 'Remember to say hello for me to the wife and children. You must bring them to see us . . . and carry yourself well.'

'God will take care of everything,' Alexis said.

'Yes, God will provide.'

After Alexis left, Estephan stared at the grey road that went past the shop, wishing he could follow it out of Consolation, past Palmiers and Colline, walking until the road ended at the sea in the North. He would walk until he wore his mind and body out from exhaustion, leaving all his defeats, frustrations, anger and pain at the roadside, wearing himself out to nothingness on the rough skin of the road.

The surveyors came soon after, knocking iron stakes into the ground, and cutting paths through the red, fragrant *ti-baume* scrub. Then came the bright, yellow bulldozers that shaved the slope as if the soil were as soft as ashes. They did not even hesitate at trees and rocks. The villagers came to watch, uncertain whether to be excited or frightened. The children welcomed the entertainment at first, with the boys all wishing to be tractor operators. Then they sensed their parents' unease and stopped coming. Even Brazil Pascal stopped going to see the transformation of his old property, although he knew it would be the last spectacle he would witness. He stayed indoors after the first week of construction and his neighbours seldom saw him again. He died one year later. Molasses protested that the decision had been his father's alone, but he maintained his distance from the older men in the village and he never ventured near Estephan St. Pierre's home.

The capital suddenly discovered Consolation, and people who had abandoned the village many years ago, began remembering their relations there. Carloads of strangers arrived at weekends, especially on Sundays, to visit old friends and relatives, to ask with agonized nonchalance about the extent and ownership of family lands, and to lavish assurances that they had never left Consolation in spirit.

The beaches at Great Hole and Little Hole were crowded again at weekends, when the young people discovered that their water was cleaner and bluer than at the other beaches they had rushed to. And to make their own beaches as comfortable as the old ones, they littered the sand with paper, bottles, cans and plastic.

Roy and Ellie Parker learned from Sylvie-James that they would not be welcomed at the home of Estephan St. Pierre with any great warmth. This disturbed Ellie greatly, but Roy was convinced that he could earn a faint mark of gratitude, if not affection, by offering to provide medical help for Estephan's urinary obstruction. Estephan welcomed him with cold politeness and waited for him to speak.

'We haven't seen you for a long time,' Roy said.

'And how's your wife? Well?' Estephan replied.

'Fine, fine, sends her love,' Roy said, and – not finding any easy way to Estephan's ear – continued, 'We have a friend who'll be coming to visit us for a couple of weeks. He's a cancer specialist . . . and I could arrange for him to see you.'

'Why? I have cancer?' Estephan asked, looking mystified.

'Well, you remember the day we went hunting? I noticed you had a lot of pain relieving yourself. At our age, prostate cancer can be a real problem. You never know. May be a good idea to have a check.'

'Um-hm,' said Estephan.

The two men sat in silence looking at the ocean that was beginning to resemble a silvery darkness, and at the yellow machines that looked like toys on the brown playground they had created.

'Well, what do you think?' Roy asked after a long silence.

'I don't know. My experiences with doctors have not been happy,' said Estephan.

'He's good . . . he's very, very good,' Roy said with anxious enthusiasm.

'I'll think about it,' Estephan said.

Roy got up to leave. 'I'll let you know when he's here,' he promised.

The surgeon came to visit, but Estephan adamantly refused to see him. He sent word that his problem was much better and that the pain was hardly noticeable. He assured them that he would be fine in a week or two. Simone urged him to see the surgeon. 'You should see somebody about your pain . . . you're keeping me awake at night with your groaning.'

'You must be hearing things,' Estephan said, and would say no more on the subject.

One night, after they had closed the shop, Estephan went to sit in the rocker on the balcony, letting the wind from the ocean wash away his own smell with the perfume of the old roses. He considered the irony of being helped by the man who had betrayed Consolation. If he agreed to see the surgeon, he would be indebted to Roy Parker; and the doctor would cut away the remnants of a manhood that another had withered thirty years ago. Estephan St. Pierre decided not to let anyone touch him.

Chapter 10

The workers clearing the trees from the site for the Parkers' resort suggested to Roy Parker that he preserve the *porier, bois d'inde* and frangipani trees. When Ellie found out that bay leaves came from the *bois d'inde trees,* she wanted to name the resort after them, but Roy pointed out that the customers would probably prefer something pronounceable and less exotic. So they called the resort *Frangipani.*

In less than a year, the construction crews had finished the cluster of white houses with pastel trim and red tile roofs. The people of Consolation said the houses looked like Christmas cakes. Then the whole was wrapped in a chain-link fence with one gateway facing the road, and another towards the beach. At each entrance, a large white sign warned:

PRIVATE PROPERTY
NO UNAUTHORIZED ENTRY

Even those villagers who were unable to read knew immediately what the signs meant. So the people stopped some distance from the fence to stare at the newcomers dressed in the polyester suits in colours that matched their houses, and wearing large, dark sunglasses so that the villagers could not tell whether they were being stared at in return. For several weeks, the fishermen of Consolation shared the beaches at Great Hole and Little Hole with the tenants of Frangipani. Then a man from the capital, dressed in the khaki uniform of a reserve policeman, told a group of children playing near the entrance to the resort, that that area of the beach was reserved for the residents of Frangipani only. A shouting match ensued, with the guard retreating behind the fence and threatening the abusive crowd with a notebook and a pencil. Word spread along the shore, and soon the bathers from the village had crowded the strip of beach fronting the hotel, while the bathers from Frangipani had moved to the opposite end of the beach. The following Sunday, Father Nantes read a notice from the Ministry of Tourism warning that the section of beach directly in front of the resort was private property, reserved for the use of the residents of Frangipani and their guests only. On Monday morning, there were four small signs on the beach repeating the warning.

The villagers came to Simone's shop to discuss the situation and to ask Estephan to intervene. 'Even when the St. Pierres owned the entire valley, they had never stopped anyone using the beaches,' they reminded Estephan.

'It's always me you want to put my foot in fire for you,' he answered, a little surprised at his own tiredness and frustration. 'What do you want me to do? Go to the capital and threaten the government?'

'But the beach is community property,' Serges protested.

'You think I don't know that?' Estephan asked. 'You think the minister who took the money to close the beach didn't know that either? Look, who's going to listen to an old man from Consolation?'

'Well, we shouldn't have invited the strangers to come here,' Madame Ferdinand said.

'Which "we"?' a man's voice said angrily. 'I never saw the people before the tractors started digging up the land. Nobody ever asked me anything about it.'

'Um-hm. Um-hm,' other voices agreed.

'Yes, yes, we know it's me you want to blame for everything. I made the lawyer come to Consolation. I told the strangers to buy his house. I told them to build their hotel. It's all my fault. If things had gone differently, you would all be kissing my backside now. It's always, "Estephan do this, Estephan do that". Well very soon I won't be causing any more trouble.'

'Ah, *Compère*, don't take it like this,' said Serges. 'Nobody could see what was going to happen. We have to take the good with the bad. Things will work out.'

Estephan's deep voice rolled slowly through the shop. 'You all thought life would never change, eh? You all thought that Consolation would always be the small quiet place it was when you were children. Well look out for yourselves. The dance is finished.'

His friends heard the new hoarseness in his voice and saw, even through the beard, that his face was sinking into the bones.

'In truth,' Maurice Jacob said, 'I don't know what anybody can do about the beach . . . but we can make their lives miserable.'

'Listen to me!' Estephan said angrily. 'Leave the people alone, the bay will take care of itself. Wait until the rainy season.'

'What's going to happen?' someone asked.

'You'll see.' Estephan replied.

The rains came in July, and it poured almost every day until November. The mangrove swamp became a brown, fetid lake, and the crabs that lived at the edges of the swamp were forced out of the flooded burrows. The crabs moved up the slope away from the beach and dug new holes in the loosened soil of the beautiful gardens at Frangipani. The chain-link fence kept out the larger crabs; so the younger ones, not having to compete with their elders, came to the resort in great crowds and established themselves with the vigour and rapacity of conquistadors. In the mornings, the residents would find their lawns perforated by deep tunnels, with the products of excavation left in piles up to one foot high.

The mosquitoes soon discovered the abundance of food and shelter at Frangipani. They raised broods of millions in the water that collected at the bottom of the crab burrows, and at night feasted on rich exotic blood. The smaller sandflies found new breeding places nearer the resort and swarmed to the evening banquets. They were so small that their presence was detected only after bites that felt like the pricks of hot needles. Residents who had not been exposed to their bites long enough to acquire tolerance found their faces swelling grotesquely and their bodies covered by large, itching blisters. The management of Frangipani issued cans of insect repellent to the residents, but the insects quickly overcame their initial reluctance to bite bodies covered with oily, uncomfortable petroleum products. The aluminium screens on doors and windows corroded rapidly from the salt sea-mist, and soon the white and pastel houses were as crowded with insects as outdoors.

Roy Parker petitioned the government to allow him to spray the swamp with insecticide, but an official in the Ministry of Agriculture and Fisheries protested that this would destroy the fishing industry along the entire east coast. The Minister of Tourism was understanding and sympathetic, related several of his own experiences with insect bites, and considered telling his remembrances of a bout of malaria during his childhood. But Roy's eyes showed his lack of interest, so the minister said goodbye. 'Please remember me to your beautiful wife.'

'Of course. Sure.' said Roy. 'Thanks for all your help, as usual.'

'Anytime, anytime,' the minister said happily.

The Parkers celebrated New Year's Eve with the security guard and one resident, whose wife had returned to the United States with a turquoise dealer from Arizona. The white and pastel houses were kept ready for guests for two more months, then Roy Parker locked the two gates and had the electricity and water supplies cut off.

Frederick Albin and Lise, now his wife, came with their two children to spend a Sunday at Consolation. The whispers that Estephan was not well had reached them.

'I hear you're telling mosquitoes whom to bite. Even telling the rain when to fall,' Frederick said to Estephan when they sat down to lunch.

For a moment, Estephan continued to chew, using the delay to decide whether he should admit that he had been as surprised as everyone else over the events that had closed the Frangipani resort. All he had hoped for was for the yellow clay on the slopes above the bay to turn into a slippery muck that would make driving virtually impossible. He smiled modestly, 'It was extraordinary. But it's exactly what I thought would happen.' He wanted to say that people should be careful not to step on the toes of a St. Pierre, but decided he did not want to hear Simone's certain response that he thought he was 'Master of Consolation'. Instead, he began boasting of the huge vegetables his garden was producing after the months of heavy rains. 'You should have seen a white yam I brought home last week. Ask Simone. The thing was so big, I had to help pull the donkey up the hill from the river. The animal groaned all the way.'

Simone groaned. Estephan glared, and continued, 'Yes, things are good here: good weather, fresh breeze. I don't know why you all want to live in the capital.'

'Well, come and see,' Frederick suggested.

'Too busy, too busy,' Estephan said in the regretful tone of one who must carry the world.

'Yes, why don't you give me some peace for a couple of days?' Simone suggested, hoping that Estephan would go to the city and perhaps be persuaded to see a doctor. By the time lunch was over, Estephan had agreed to visit the capital – because they had dared him to.

The driver of the early-morning bus to the capital, the *Advancement,* was flattered that Estephan St. Pierre had chosen to travel on his bus, and insisted that Estephan sit at the front with him. Estephan protested, although he had come to expect those courtesies, but allowed himself to be persuaded. In fact, he had had no intention of sitting elsewhere. He felt slightly guilty about leaving, and while the bus was loading other passengers and produce for the town market, he tried to hide his discomfort behind repeated instructions to Simone. She nodded indulgently until the bus moved off; and when it stopped again, at the bottom of the hill near Madame Ferdinand's home, Estephan looked back to see Simone walking back to the shop, leaving him with the small resentment that she could manage without him.

Frederick Albin met him at the bus depot. 'You're well?' he asked in greeting, 'And Simone?'

'What to do? What to do? We'll survive,' Estephan replied, and because it was expected, described the hazards and miseries of travel by bus. 'Look at me, covered with charcoal dust and smelling of diesel smoke. All my body is hurting.'

Frederick nodded in agreement and sympathy, '... smelling of diesel smoke. And it is such a long trip, and they pack so many people into the bus. It's a good thing you didn't come by the afternoon bus.'

'Yes, that heat can kill you,' Estephan said.

Estephan spent the rest of the day in the small pharmacy with Frederick and Lise, listening to stories about Guy Chalon, who had died three years before. Estephan stared in fascination at the people who crowded the sidewalks, dressed in clothes he thought were bizarre or immodest. The two children stared in equal fascination at the tall, bearded man who had given each a dollar, and who looked so much like Father Christmas.

On the second night of his visit, Lise awoke suddenly from sleep and shook Frederick by the shoulder. 'Frederick! Wake up! I didn't hear Estephan come back from the toilet.'

'That's what you woke me for? Maybe you were sleeping.'

'Um-um. No, no. Something's wrong. Go and see. Go on.'

Frederick could hear the moans before he got to the toilet door. 'Estephan. You're sick?' he called softly.

'I have trouble passing water. I'll be fine in a little while,' Estephan replied.

'You've seen a doctor?' Frederick asked.

'Those people have never done anything good for me.'

'But maybe you should see somebody while you're in town,' Frederick insisted.

'Um,' Estephan said, and Frederick did not know whether he had moaned or assented.

'You'll be all right?' Frederick asked.

'Yes, yes, I'm OK now.'

When Frederick got back into bed, Lise was waiting. 'What was it?'

'Estephan has trouble passing water. I asked him to go and see a doctor, but he is so hard-headed.'

'You think I should talk to him?' Lise asked.

'And you expect St. Pierre to listen to a young woman?'

The next morning, Lise Albin knocked softly on Estephan's door. 'Coffee,' she said.

Lise brought into the room the smells of forest water when the rain has just fallen, of the little streams in the hills above Consolation, and of the wind that blows from the ocean and up the valley of St. Pierre. At that moment, Estephan grew so homesick for his little village only two hours away by bus, that he resolved to do anything Frederick asked, just so that he could return home quickly.

'Mr. Estephan,' Lise said, 'Frederick said you're not well. He believes you should see a doctor.'

After a frightening silence, Estephan looked at the girl he wished was his daughter. 'You wouldn't let me say no, eh?'

'No.' said Lise.

The young doctor who examined him was so solicitous that Estephan wondered whether he was a real doctor. He asked about Estephan's family, told about his, joked about the escapades of his three-year-old daughter, and related his experiences as a medical student abroad.

After his examination, he waited for Estephan to dress before he spoke. 'You have a very enlarged prostate, Mr. St. Pierre. I hate to tell you that, but you have to have surgery to ease the pain in your bladder. And we'll have to take a look and see if there's anything else going on.'

Estephan nodded in resignation. 'I know,' he said.

Five days later, Simone and several of the older villagers accompanied Estephan to the hospital. The next day, Maurice Jacob and Serges Jean-Baptiste returned to see him. The two men sat near the bed, with their hats on their knees, searching for things to say to help their friend's attempts at apologising for his helplessness. Maurice was relieved when he noticed the urinary catheter that had been inserted to empty Estephan's bladder.

'Now what's that tube you have there?' Maurice asked.

'To pass water.'

'So tell me,' Maurice asked with much wonder, 'you were not satisfied with what God gave you, so you came to the hospital for a longer one?'

'Maurice!' Serges said in protest, 'You cannot make jokes about things like that. You never have any respect for anybody. Now watch your mouth for once. I tell . . .'

'Let Estephan talk for himself,' Maurice replied. 'Good, now tell us, Estephan, how you are going to walk around with that long thing?'

'What to do,' said Estephan. 'I was so glad when they put that thing in, that I don't care if they want me to keep it. They're operating on me tomorrow.'

The surgeon removed some of the constricting tissue, enough to provide Estephan with temporary relief. He waited until the next day, when Estephan was alone with Simone, to talk to them. 'A cancer has spread from the prostate and we will not be able to take it all out. It went on for too long. Believe me, it hurts me very much to tell you that.'

Estephan St. Pierre continued to work for another year, then one night he said to Simone after a quiet dinner, 'I can't take it again. The body . . . it's tired.'

Simone nodded, then began to cry silently.

Soon, his friends had to help him up the small incline to the house. He insisted that Simone needed him, and he could not sit around on the balcony doing nothing. Bertrand Louis came every night. Except when it rained. The others said that was because the old house he had bought from Madame Ferdinand was so decrepit, he had to stay home to place pans to catch the water that ignored the roof.

One Saturday in June, the men were sitting in Simone's shop calling out to passengers getting off the evening bus from the city. Bertrand watched the conductor hand down a bicycle from the luggage rack.

'When I used to live in the city,' he said, his eyes calling back faces from a time that he did not revisit often, 'there was a small bar where I used to stop sometimes. For a little something. There was one man, his name was Gaston. Well, Gaston never ever had enough to pay for his drinks. But the owner would accept what Gaston had, and he would write down how much Gaston owed. Every month, he would refuse to let Gaston have even a glass of water until he paid. So next day, Gaston would arrive with enough to pay all he owed, then the whole thing would start all over again.

'But one day, Gaston stopped coming. A few days later, we saw him riding past the bar. Riding so slow, that we didn't understand why the bike didn't fall. So the bar owner rushed to the door and shouted to him, "Gaston! Pay me my money!" But Gaston kept looking straight ahead, and the bicycle cruised by as slow as a hearse, going 'tick . . . tick . . . tick . . .' and, as he passed, he shouted, "No brakes! No brakes! Can't stop!"'

'So why didn't the owner just grab Gaston?' Serges asked.

'And leave us alone in the bar? We were serious drinkers.'

'So what happened?' Estephan asked.

'Well, you see,' Bertrand said, 'his wife got tired of all

his drinking and she used to stop at the corner near the bar – with a stick. And she promised to beat him – in the street – if she ever saw him even stop to talk to us.'

'So his wife, she was a large lady?' Simone asked.

'No, no,' said Bertrand. 'She was small, just five feet tall, and her husband must have weighed about two hundred and fifty pounds. But her tongue was as sharp as a fish bone, and she was afraid of nothing. And of nobody. If Gaston had been brave enough to beat her, he would never have slept safely again.'

They nodded sympathetically, then Serges said, 'That's like Madame Hippolyte's daughter and the schoolmaster at Palmiers.'

'What happened?' Bertrand asked

'Well, Madame Hippolyte had two children, a boy and a girl. The girl was eleven years old when they built the school, but she said she was too old to go to school. So she worked the land with her parents. The boy was eight years old and they sent him to school. One day, the parents wanted help with bagging copra, so they sent the girl to the school to ask them to send the boy home early. The girl asked the headmaster, in the little English she knew, "Mammy-us tell you, when it is three half-past, send he for she." The schoolmaster forgot that the poor child had never been to school and did not speak much English, so he grabbed her by the arm and said, "What kind of language is that? When you speak to me, speak correctly." She bit him. He slapped her. That's when war broke out. It took the other teachers ten minutes to get her off the schoolmaster. When she was finished, his left ear was torn, one eye was closed, two teeth were missing and his shirt was gone. The teachers could have stopped the fight sooner, but they had to hold back her brother. And they were enjoying too much the sight of the headmaster running around the school and the little girl chasing him, spitting out curses and his hair.'

After some reflection, Maurice said, 'Now let me tell you about a story I heard about a man from the country who went to look for a woman in The Market.'

'A true story?' Serges asked.

'I don't know. I wasn't there, but I think so.'

'Um-hm,' they agreed.

'Good,' Maurice said, and continued, 'This man waited until one o'clock in the morning because he didn't want to pay too much money. Eventually, he saw this most beautiful woman standing just out of the light. When he got near, she smiled. He asked her quickly, "The way is clear for me?" She nodded and signalled for him to follow. So they went into some bushes. But it was a full moon and he was in a hurry to finish before somebody came by and saw them. So he bent down to take off his pants, and he heard the woman laugh. He looked up quickly, and it was then he noticed that her face was as white as ashes and she had two long fangs in her mouth . . . like a cat.'

'Like a cat?' Serges asked.

'Serges!' Estephan said impatiently.

'Wait, wait, I'm not finished.' Maurice said, and continued, 'Well the man grabbed his pants and ran, and didn't stop until he was in the middle of the city, near the wharf. And there was an old man walking slowly along the street. So the man ran up to him to relate what he had just seen. When he had finished, the old man said, "Long fangs? Like these?" And he opened his mouth and there were two teeth even longer than the woman's.'

'It was *la diablesse.*' Serges said with certainty.

'Um-hm.' Maurice agreed.

'Idiots!' said Estephan.

'So, Estephan,' Maurice asked, 'You never had anything strange happen to you in the city?'

Estephan shook his head and let the smoke from his pipe drift slowly away to anoint his friends, then climb contentedly towards the old beams of the roof.

'How about the time you went to town in your tight pants?' Simone asked.

'What are you talking about, woman? You didn't even know me then.'

'Yes, but you told me about it,' Simone said.

'Eh-eh, but you will have to tell us about that, Estephan. What do you say, Bertrand?' Maurice said, and his mouth remained open in anticipation.

'Just before the war,' Estephan said, and his voice rumbled like thunder that was far away and not frightening, 'I went to town for the christening of my cousin's child. After church, as we were walking home, a bunch of little boys started following us and started shouting, "Boom-boom-boom! Boom-boom-boom!" My relatives started walking faster and faster, and I followed . . . until we were almost running through the town. With people laughing at us . . . I was wearing these old pants – that looked like gun barrels. I didn't go back to the city for years; I was afraid someone would remember my face.'

'You should have kept the pants. That's what people are wearing now,' Serges said.

'Children can be so wicked,' Bertrand said sadly.

'If!' said Maurice in agreement, thinking of the torment he had visited upon Courbée the leper, until she told him she could see the signs of her disease in his face.

'But wait! Let me tell you about Patrice . . .' Estephan continued.

'Which Patrice?' Maurice interrupted.

'You don't know him. Man in the capital,' Estephan said impatiently and continued, 'Anyway, Patrice decided he wanted to be a policeman so he could walk around town swinging a stick and bullying people. So he lied his way into the police training school, but after one week he decided to be a prison warder instead. Eventually Patrice became a warder, and misery came and sat on his shoulders and refused to leave. Eh! In two days, Patrice found out that almost every prisoner was a friend or a relative or an acquaintance.

'After two months of being blackmailed, doing favours, carrying messages and smuggling food and cigarettes, he decided that God had not made him to take that kind of punishment. It was worse than the suffering of the thieves and assassins he was taking care of. But he didn't know how to get out unless he was disabled. One night he was climbing the long iron stairs up from the cells when he found a way to get out of his trouble. He got to the top and threw himself down the stairs.

'They found him the next morning, calling for help and groaning his head off. He couldn't walk or even lift his arm. They said the only part of him that was not broken or cut was the skin behind his left ear.'

'The man did that?' Bertrand asked in disbelief.

'That's what I heard ' Estephan replied.

'That is something,' Maurice said appreciatively and repeated the parts of the story that he found especially appealing. 'So he missed only a small piece behind his ear?' he asked, thinking of the embellishments he would add to the story when he would retell it later.

Each of the old friends spoke slowly, to delay the end of their stories, and to consider each word before it was spoken, to be sure it was the right one. For a reason that they all felt, it had become important to tell all their stories, and to repeat over and over again the history of Consolation, as each remembered it. It was almost midnight when they got up to leave.

Bertrand Louis stayed to help Simone close the shop. Serges and Maurice helped Estephan to the balcony. He would sit there and wait for Simone. A few minutes later, he watched Simone approaching, lighting the way with a small kerosene lamp. It was too late now to say all the things a man should have said to a woman, and she would probably be embarrassed. She had not protested all the years of his arrogance and inattention. Instead, she had ensured that his clothes were washed and his food was ready. Like one of his arms, she had been necessary. Now they were both too old to talk of love. As he watched Simone walking stiffly, lifting her feet high over the rough ground, Estephan St. Pierre at last admitted to himself that he had always loved his wife. He did not have to say anything to her now, it was as it should be – Bertrand would look after Simone, and Serges would look after Maurice.

Consolation would change, with or without him. He was already considered a nuisance by the younger villagers. Other strangers would come, and luck and old men would not be enough to protect the old ways of doing things. Most of all, he wanted revenge on the crab that crawled with impunity through his insides. This time he would win. When he died, the crab would die with him. There would be no more pain, no more fighting, no more worrying about rain or people's problems. He just wished he were not so afraid to die.

Father Nantes came to visit during the week and Estephan asked to make his confession. 'I don't think I'll be troubling you again,' he said to the priest.

'Don't say that,' Father Nantes said, 'you're just tired.'

When Estephan began his confession, the priest forced himself to listen to the words of a popular song that were coming from a neighbour's radio, so that he would not hear the old man's words. He wanted all the myths that surrounded Estephan St. Pierre to be true, and when the people of Consolation would boast of him, there would be no shadows of half-remembered sins to dim the light of their stories.

On Friday night, Simone awoke suddenly when Estephan's soft moaning stopped. She looked up to see him going through the door into the darkness outside.

'Estephan,' she called, 'where are you going? You don't even have a light.'

He turned around to look at her and said with regret, 'I'm sorry . . . I'm going now.' Then he went out.

She sat up to go and persuade him to come back inside, when she brushed against the cold body next to her. She jumped out of bed, too frightened to scream, but eventually she managed to light the small votive lamp above the bed. The door was locked, and Estephan's body lay on the bed, his eyes fixed on the darkness above.

Simone went onto the balcony to sit near the old roses to wait for morning. She could not understand how she could have seen him so clearly in the dark, and she did not understand why she had heard him say he was sorry. She had been the wife of the most important man in Consolation; he had taken care of her, had never shamed her with a mistress, and had provided enough to make her comfortable. She thanked God that he had never discovered the infidelity that was still too frightening to recall.

The wake for Estephan St. Pierre lasted for two days. The people of Consolation came to drink coffee and rum, and one by one to offer their songs and their stories as hosannas to the man who had carried them, bandaged their injuries, settled their disputes and protected them. He had been the land and their father and their brother. Simone St. Pierre watched them all through a white flame of tears, hearing Estephan's voice saying over and over, 'I'm going now . . .'

Three days after the funeral, a rainstorm swept through the valley. It was so severe that the villagers swore that heaven was no longer able to ignore the grief of Consolation, and had cried to admit its sorrow. It did not rain again for four months. The small stream that supplied the village with drinking water dried up completely, so that the villagers had to walk three miles to the St. Pierre River to carry back water that was brown with mud and with tannin from rotting leaves. The deep greens of the valley turned brown, then grey, as the trees lost their leaves. A few cactuses and succulent plants near the seashore, which had protected their green stems from the cows and sheep with thorns and poisonous latex, disappeared one night when they were discovered by starving goats.

The air over the valley was filled with the resinous smells of dried *ti-baume* shrubs and the sulphurous, metallic vapours of baked rock and earth. Great cracks that appeared to be bottomless appeared in the ground, and stories spread of children and animals that had disappeared into the dark crevices. The streams that had tarnished the sea with silt stopped flowing, and the water at Great Hole became clearer. Its blues and greens, no longer having to compete with the brilliance of a wet green earth, shone with such defiant beauty that people driving through St. Pierre stopped to marvel, and to wonder at the pastel-coloured houses of Frangipani.

On a Saturday night in October, the people of St. Pierre heard the tender drumming of heavy raindrops on their roofs. The rain continued every night and morning for the next week, and the brown earth turned green so quickly that the villagers could not remember whether the grass had ever disappeared.

The small stream that ran through Consolation swelled with brown water as it scoured and rinsed its banks, taking down to the bay dead leaves, empty tin cans, plastic containers, crushed cardboard boxes and kitchen refuse. After the rains stopped, the stream cleared, and the sound of its hurrying, hurrying down the valley, over fallen logs and the black rocks of its bed, sent the children of Consolation to sleep.

In the few weeks before the trees leafed again, the pastel-coloured houses of Frangipani, looking like toy houses on a green carpet, could be seen easily from the road; and government officials came and admired the bay and the abandoned resort, frowning importantly and nodding seriously. If one listened carefully, one heard the important men say things like:

'Basic infrastructure already in place . . .'

'Fuller utilisation of resources . . .'

'Needed economic diversity . . .'
'Development!'
The villagers looked on warily, apprehensive about the pretty houses near the bay that had brought them flood and drought. The government officials went back to the capital to make great plans for golf courses, tennis courts, riding paths, and swimming pools next to the ocean.

On the Sunday that followed the end of the drought, Bertrand Louis walked Simone St. Pierre home after mass. The following Sunday, he accompanied her to church. Neither noticed when their weekly meetings became a habit. On the anniversary of Estephan's death, as they walked home from church, Simone touched his arm lightly. 'You'll stop for a little eggnog?' she asked.

'Good. I wouldn't say no,' Bertrand said. 'These days, the old body has to rest itself more often. My feet hurt so much.'

Simone nodded and said, 'You can put your shoes under my bed you know . . . whenever you're ready.'

For several seconds neither spoke, nor dared look at the other; then Simone entered the small balcony that fronted her house and stood waiting for Bertrand to follow. Bertrand Louis went to the rocking-chair near the old roses, and for several minutes he stared at the dark-blue surface of the ocean that distance had pressed smooth, and at the flawless cut of the horizon. Then his gaze came back up the valley, over the red leaves of the *ti-baume* shrubs, and up the small path that led from Great Hole to the road that passed close by. He bent over to untie the laces of the black leather shoes that he wore only at mass and at funerals.

Simone St. Pierre moved to the door. 'Come inside,' she said.

Other Titles in the Longman Caribbean Writers Series

Homestretch

Velma Pollard

David and Edith are happy to return home to Jamaica after spending several dreary years living in England, and their niece, Laura, is delighted to see them again. But for Laura's friend, Brenda, who is also returning home – 'to find herself' – the adjustment to life in the Caribbean is not so smooth.

Velma Pollard sensitively captures the mixed emotions of homecoming. In *Homestretch* she skilfully unravels the life stories of her characters, interweaving the plot with vivid, almost tangible, descriptions of Jamaican life past and present.

Velma Pollard is a Senior Lecturer in Language Education at the University of the West Indies, as well as a prizewinning novelist.

ISBN 0582 22732 1

DreamStories

Kamau Brathwaite

A distinguished poet, cultural historian and essayist, Kamau Brathwaite is widely regarded as one of the Caribbean's most original contemporary writers. A contributor to the *Longman Caribbean Writers* anthology of oral and written verse, *Voiceprint,* his extensive body of published work also includes *X/Self, The Arrivants* and *Middle Passages.*

Through the shimmering and elusive oneiric narratives that make up *DreamStories,* Brathwaite courageously creates fiction from a marriage of personal trauma and the wider social upheavals and tragic episodes that have shaped the history of the Caribbean. In so doing, he confronts, challenges and subverts the conventions of storytelling and language use, setting words free of traditional structures. His only companion in this descent into the maelstrom of personal and cultural memory is a computer, used to create visual effects to convey nuances of meaning, or – as he describes it – to 'create word sculpture on the page, word sculpture in the ear.'

Like any dream, Brathwaite's dream journeys are not always easy to chart – though they always pass through exhilarating landscapes – but an introduction by Gordon Rohlehr provides readers with an illuminating map.

ISBN 0582 09340 6

Karl and other stories

Velma Pollard

A varied and enchanting collection of eight stories by Velma Pollard, the author of the novel *Homestretch.* All the stories – set in Canada and Jamaica – are carefully and beautifully crafted and reveal to great effect the sensitivity and humour of Velma Pollard's writing.

Centrepiece of the collection is the novella, *Karl*, which won the Casa de las Americas literary prize in 1992. This describes a young man's encounter with the nuances and complexities of life among middle-class Jamaican society.

ISBN 0582 22726 7

Between Two Seasons

I J Boodhoo

Manu has an obsession – to play 'diable' in the Trinidad carnival. This leads him into conflict with his wife, Samdaye, and sets in motion a train of events that threatens to destroy the lives of family and neighbours.

Interwoven with the story of how Manu and Samdaye cope with adversity, is the theme of the economic and judicial injustice suffered by plantation workers.

This compelling tale is the first novel of Isaiah James Boodhoo, a Trinidadian with an established international reputation as a painter.

ISBN 0582 22869 7

The Lonely Londoners

Sam Selvon

In the 1950s, thousands of West Indians emigrated to Britain in the search for an assured and prosperous future. They left behind more than sunshine and had worse than cold and rain to contend with. Sam Selvon – who died in 1994 – relates the harsh realities of poor housing, low-status jobs and racism that so often became the cornerstones of life in the chilly drabness of postwar London. With sharp observation, wit and an ear for the music of ordinary conversation, Selvon tells the story of the privations endured by these new Londoners, their friendships and resilience.

. . . *the definitive novel about London's West Indians.*
FINANCIAL TIMES

. . . *a vernacular comedy of pathos.*
THE GUARDIAN

ISBN 0582 64264 7

Ways of Sunlight

Sam Selvon

A sparkling collection of vignettes told with humour and sensitivity. While some affectionately explore corners of rural life in Trinidad, others relate the depression of hard times in London – hustling for survival while consigned to living in the city's cold, damp basements, accommodation seemingly reserved for those not yet regarded as proper citizens of the capital.

Mr Selvon writes naturally in dialogue, he never lets the pace sag and he suggests a scene with a telling economy of means.
TIMES LITERARY SUPPLEMENT

ISBN 0582 64261 2

Longman Caribbean Writers

Consolation	EG Long	0 582 23913 3
Between Two Seasons	I J Boodhoo	0 582 22869 7
Satellite City	A McKenzie	0 582 08688 4
Karl and Other Stories	V Pollard	0 582 22726 7
Homestretch	V Pollard	0 582 22732 1
Discoveries	J Wickham	0 582 21804 7
The Chieftain's Carnival	M Anthony	0 582 21805 5
DreamStories	K Brathwaite	0 582 09340 6
Arrival of the Snakewoman	O Senior	0 582 03170 2
Summer Lightning	O Senior	0 582 78627 4
The Dragon Can't Dance	E Lovelace	0 582 64231 0
Ways of Sunlight	S Selvon	0 582 64261 2
The Lonely Londoners	S Selvon	0 582 64264 7
A Brighter Sun	S Selvon	0 582 64265 5
Foreday Morning	S Selvon	0 582 03982 7
In the Castle of my Skin	G Lamming	0 582 64267 1
My Bones and My Flute	E Mittelholzer	0 582 78552 9
Black Albino	N Roy	0 582 78563 4
The Children of Sisyphus	O Patterson	0 582 78571 5
The Jumbie Bird	I Khan	0 582 78619 3
Plays for Today	E Hill *et al*	0 582 78620 7
Old Story Time and Smile Orange	T. D. Rhone	0 582 78633 9
Baby Mother and the King of Swords	L Goodison	0 582 05492 3
Two Roads to Mount Joyful	E McKenzie	0 582 07125 9
Voiceprint	S Brown *et al*	0 582 78629 0

Other Titles Available

Longman African Writers

Title	Author	ISBN
The Surrender and Other Stories	Mabel Segun	0 582 25833 2
Sozaboy	K Saro-Wiwa	0 582 23699 1
Tides	I Okpewho	0 582 10276 6
Of Men and Ghosts	K Aidoo	0 582 22871 9
Flowers and Shadows	B Okri	0 582 03536 8
Violence	F Iyayi	0 582 00240 0
The Victims	I Okpewho	0 582 00241 9
Call Me Not a Man	M Matshoba	0 582 00242 7
The Beggar's Strike	A Sowfall	0 582 00243 5
Dilemma Of a Ghost/Anowa	A A Aidoo	0 582 00244 3
Our Sister Killjoy	A A Aidoo	0 582 00391 1
No Sweetness Here	A A Aidoo	0 582 00393 8
The Marriage of Anansewa/Edufa	E Sutherland	0 582 00245 1
The Cockroach Dance	M Mwangi	0 582 00392 X
Muriel At Metropolitan	A Tlali	0 582 01657 6
Children of Soweto	M Mzamane	0 582 01680 0
A Son Of The Soil	W Katiyo	0 582 02656 3
The Stillborn	Z Alkali	0 582 02657 1
The Life of Olaudah Equiano	P Edwards	0 582 03070 6
Sundiata	D T Niane	0 582 64259 0
The Last Duty	I Okpewho	0 582 78535 9
Hungry Flames	M Mzamane	0 582 78590 1
Scarlet Song	M Ba	0 582 78595 2
Fools and Other Stories	N Ndebele	0 582 78621 5
Master and Servant	D Mulwa	0 582 78632 0
The Park	J Matthews	0 582 04080 9
Man Pass Man	N Mokoso	0 582 01681 9
Loyalties	A Maja-Pearce	0 582 78628 2
Sugarcane With Salt	James Ng'ombe	0 582 05204 1
Hurricane of Dust	Amu Djoleto	0 582 01682 7
Study Guide to 'Scarlet Song'	M Ba	0 582 21979 5

All these titles are available or can be ordered from your local bookseller. For further information on these titles, and on study guides available, contact your local Longman agent or Longman International Education, Longman Group Limited, Longman House, Burnt Mill, Harlow, Essex, CM20 2JE, England.